ULTIMATE
SLOW COOKER

TOP 100
taste.COM.AU

ULTIMATE SLOW COOKER

THE BEST OF THE BEST RECIPES FROM AUSTRALIA'S #1 FOOD SITE

HarperCollinsPublishers

CONTENTS

HELLO!

Whenever we start talking about slow cooker recipes at taste HQ you can almost hear everyone drooling. We're huge fans of the humble appliance that can, well, just make life so much easier. We're all time-poor in this busy world, and the marvellous slow cooker offers the benefit of set-and-forget cooking – just pile everything into the pot in the morning and come home hungry after a busy day to a delicious, aromatic and heartwarming meal. The even better bit? Slow cooking is also an easy way of bringing out the rich flavours and tender textures of your favourite meals.

And it's not just the flavour we love. We're on board for the minimal prep required too.

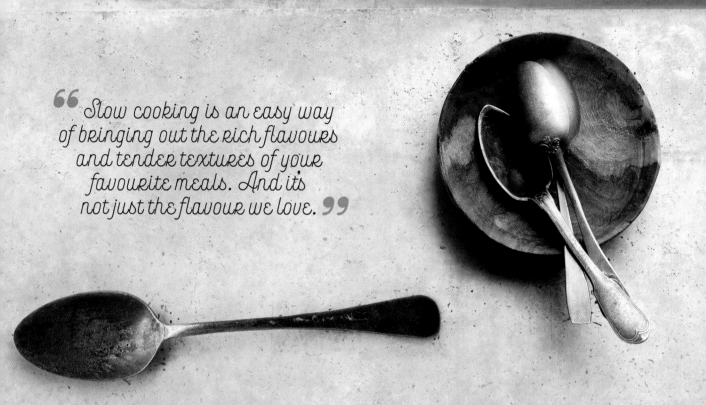

"Slow cooking is an easy way of bringing out the rich flavours and tender textures of your favourite meals. And it's not just the flavour we love."

In fact, you'll find an at-a-glance prep time on each recipe page in *Ultimate Slow Cooker*. There's also a key guide for one pots, gluten free, vegetarian and vegan options. Plus, we have you covered year round with slow cooker ideas for all seasons – our super salads, summer curries, sweet bakes and more will have you whipping out the slow cooker at any time. And check out our ideas for slow cooker sides – clever options to make the most of fresh produce while your main meal is cooking.

We've also included secret hacks that our foodies use and love in their own cooking. Look out for them throughout the book – there are shortcuts for saving money and time,

ideas for making it vego, and tips on how to batch cook and freeze for another meal.

Every recipe uses ingredients that are at your local supermarket to make planning and cooking affordable and simple. Plus, every recipe is tried, tested, trusted and rated by the millions of people who use and review taste.com.au recipes every month.

So sit back, choose your favourite recipes and let the slow cooker do the work for you!

Cassie

**CASSIE MERCER,
GROUP COMMISSIONING EDITOR**

HOW TO USE
ULTIMATE
SLOW COOKER

Welcome to taste.com.au's *Ultimate Slow Cooker*, with all the recipes, tips, tricks and hacks you need to create this winter's best comfort food.

AMAZING FEATURES

Full prep & cooking times

Complete nutritional information

Secret Hack

At-a-glance prep time

5-star recipe ratings

Reviews from home cooks

KEY GUIDES
Highlighted dots indicating gluten-free, one-pot, vegan, make-ahead, freezable and year-round faves

COOK'S NOTE
Helpful hints and insider knowledge courtesy of our expert food team

INFO AT A GLANCE

Use the icons to find the best choices for you and your family (such as vegan, one pot, gluten free, freezable – or maybe all four at once – and more). Just follow the highlighted dots, or turn to our index, which starts on page 246.

● FREEZABLE ● GLUTEN FREE ● MAKE AHEAD ○ ONE POT ○ VEGAN ○ VEGO ● YEAR-ROUND FAVE

SECRET HACKS

Our insider tips will save time, money or help you adapt for dietary needs.

Secret Hack
Budget saver! Replace the pork shoulder with 2kg of chicken drumsticks.

CRUNCH THE NUMBERS

Nutritional panels help you track your calories and calculate your protein, carbs and fat, so you make informed meal choices for you and your family.

NUTRITION (PER SERVE)

CAL	FAT	SAT FAT	PROTEIN	CARBS
216	7g	2g	14g	18g

FRESH SIDES

Use the best of the season to create delicious side dishes for your slow-cooked meals. These stress-free and speedy recipe ideas range from roast cabbage and crispy baked vegies to zingy salads and fruit-filled accompaniments.

THE TASTE.COM.AU GUARANTEE →

All taste.com.au recipes are triple-tested, rated and reviewed by Aussie cooks just like you. Plus, every ingredient is as close as your local supermarket.

ALL YOU NEED TO KNOW ABOUT
Slow Cookers

Dinner is easy when you slow down! Food director Michelle Southan shows you how to create delicious meals using your slow cooker.

The slow cooker took off in the early 1970s and has had a revival in recent years – and it's easy to see why. It makes flavoursome meals with minimal fuss and is a lifesaver for busy people. While the cooking time is long, the preparation is fast and easy, so you can set the slow cooker to Low and let it bubble away while you're at work or pottering around the house. As a bonus, slow cookers help you save money, too: they work best with cheaper cuts of meat and use less energy than an oven.

What is a slow cooker?
This electrical appliance usually features a heatproof ceramic bowl inserted into a metal outer casing. Low, even heat from the side allows the food inside to maintain a gentle simmer over a period of several hours, which creates tender, aromatic dishes.

Buying a slow cooker
Slow cookers are available from department stores and kitchenware outlets in sizes from 3.5L to 6.5L, and prices start from about $30 up to $150. Most slow cookers have Low and High settings, while some also have a timer that clicks to "keep warm" mode when the food is ready. For safety and convenience, look for features such as a glass lid, cool-touch handles, a dishwasher-safe removable insert, and a removable cord so you can serve the food at the table straight out of the slow cooker.

Cleaning your slow cooker
Follow the manufacturer's recommendations for cleaning your slow cooker. Ensure you don't use abrasive cleaners, steel wool or scouring pads as these can damage the surfaces and non-stick coating. Use a soft cloth and a mild detergent to wash out the ceramic bowl of the slow cooker. If the bowl is dishwasher safe, you can clean it that way. The exterior of the appliance, usually brushed stainless steel, can be wiped over with a soft, damp cloth and then dried thoroughly with a tea towel.

HOW TO USE A SLOW COOKER
A guide to times
In general, slow cookers are forgiving with cooking times – it's unlikely that an hour or two over the suggested cooking time will affect the final product. For best results, keep the lid on the slow cooker during the cooking process and try not to lift it too often, otherwise steam will escape and the temperature inside the slow cooker will drop. To convert your favourite cool-weather recipes, such as stews and curries, from conventional cooking methods to the slow cooker, adjust the cooking times following the chart opposite and see our slow cooker know-how tips below.

Slow cooker know-how
For slow-cooking success and good food safety, follow these tips:
• Cut all the ingredients into similar-sized pieces so that they cook evenly.
• Thaw frozen meat, poultry or vegetables before cooking. Slow cookers take too long to reach a safe temperature for frozen food.
• When adding dried spices or spice mixes, it's best to cook them at the same time as you're browning and caramelising your ingredients, or the spices will not release their full flavour and aroma.
• Prepare ingredients the night before and store in the fridge in a container. Don't put the slow cooker bowl in the fridge, or it won't heat up quickly enough to stop bacteria growing.
• Fill your slow cooker between half and three-quarters full so the food cooks evenly.
• Use about ½-1 cup less liquid than for other cooking methods. Air circulates in the cooker, creating steam, which adds more liquid.
• Remove cooked food from the slow cooker bowl before placing in the fridge. The insert is designed to retain heat, so it won't cool quickly enough to stop bacteria growing.
• Don't reheat slow-cooked meals in your slow cooker – it takes too long to reach a safe temperature.

COOKING TIMES
How to convert recipes for a slow cooker and a conventional oven

If you want to cook your favourite slow cooker recipe, but would like to speed things up and cook it in a conventional oven, the main thing to take into account is that you will need to increase the liquid by about a ½ cup to 1 cup.

Alternatively, to convert your favourite casserole, stew or curry to the slow cooker, decrease the liquid by ½-1 cup. Follow this general guide to cooking times:

Oven or stovetop	Slow cooker (High setting)	Slow cooker (Low setting)
15 – 30 minutes	1½ – 2½ hours	4 – 6 hours
30 – 45 minutes	2 – 3 hours	6 – 8 hours
45 minutes – 3 hours	4 – 6 hours	8 – 12 hours

TIPS, TRICKS AND HACKS FROM THE TASTE TEAM

With a few clever tricks, your slow cooker could save you even more time this winter. We've rounded up the best ever slow-cooker secrets from the taste team experts and readers.

Cook two meals at once

Taste's senior producer Rebecca was blown away when she saw a friend fill one oven bag with a vegetarian bean chilli and another with Mexican beef before cooking them together in the slow cooker. Two meals, one session!

Soak up the condensation

Taste reader Jenny says she puts a tea towel under the slow cooker lid to catch water and stop the stew thinning too much.

Convert oven recipes to slow cooker

To make your slow cooker recipe suitable for the oven and vice versa, all you have to do is tweak the time and add or remove some of the liquid. You'll find our handy conversion guide on page 11.

Spray the bowl

Taste reader Sue reveals she always sprays her slow cooker bowl with olive oil spray before loading ingredients, which makes it much easier to wash at the end.

Buy meat on the bone

The taste foodies say using meat on the bone will give you even more flavour in your sauce. Bone-in chicken thighs or drumsticks are more suitable than breasts, while a lamb shoulder will make for a tastier stew than backstrap.

Brown, always

Taste reader Sheryl says she always browns meat before adding to the slow cooker, saying: "It adds more flavour and looks better, too."

Add cornflour

Coating the meat in cornflour before browning it and transferring it to the slow cooker helps thicken the sauce, says taste reader Jo.

Add citrus

Taste reader Donna recommends adding mandarin peel to meat dishes, explaining: "It's a natural tenderiser."

Do the dream clean

"I used to hate cleaning my slow cooker," says taste reader Danielle, until she worked out that she could add soap and water to it and leave it cooking on Low for half an hour or so. "It pulls off all the crust stuck to the sides and makes it really easy to wash later," she says.

Layer roasts

Taste reader Wendy says that she batch-cooks the same types of meat to save on time, effort and power. For example, put "pork shoulder on the bottom for pulled pork and place pork belly on top of it. The belly can be taken out early and crisped up under the grill." One cooking session, several different meals!

Use up leftovers

Senior online editor Laura loves using slow-cooked leftovers to make pies and freezes them for later. "Pretty much anything you slow cook can make a pie filling – especially if you have a pie maker or muffin pan," she says.

Be safe with legumes

Digital producer Rosie says: "Adding legumes to your crockpot? Boil dried lentils and beans for 10 minutes before adding to the slow cooker, because some legumes contain toxins that aren't destroyed when cooked at low temperatures."

Make an onion layer

Add a layer of sliced onions under the meat you're cooking in the slow cooker so it doesn't stick, says taste reader Adamina. The onion also adds flavour.

ROASTS

THESE MELT-IN-THE-MOUTH CLASSICS WITH
A TWIST WILL INSPIRE AND DELIGHT EVERYONE.

BEEF AND LEMONGRASS
POT ROAST

A selection of Asian spices helps to make this roast even more special.
Serve with pumpkin, plus steamed greens for added crunch.

SERVES 6   **PREP** 20 mins   **COOK** 6 hours 10 mins

3 tsp peanut oil
800g beef blade roast
6 French shallots, peeled
2 garlic cloves, thinly sliced, halved
4cm piece fresh ginger, peeled,
    finely grated
1 tbs tomato paste
330ml (1⅓ cups) beef stock
80ml (⅓ cup) Chinese cooking wine
2 tbs brown sugar
2 tsp soy sauce
2 carrots, diagonally sliced
1 lemongrass stem, pale section
    only, trimmed, quartered
2 star anise
Mashed pumpkin and steamed
    broccolini, to serve

1 Heat 1 tsp oil in a large deep non-stick frying pan over medium-high heat. Season beef. Add to pan. Cook, turning occasionally, for 8 minutes or until browned all over. Transfer to the slow cooker.

2 Reduce heat to medium. Heat remaining oil in pan. Add shallots. Cook, stirring, for 4 minutes or until softened. Add garlic, ginger and tomato paste. Cook, stirring, for 1 minute. Add stock, wine, sugar and soy. Stir. Pour over beef. Add carrot, lemongrass and star anise. Cover and cook on Low for 6 hours or until beef is tender.

3 Remove and discard lemongrass stem and star anise. Slice the beef. Serve beef with mashed pumpkin and steamed broccolini.

COOK'S NOTE

Chinese cooking wine is available in the Asian section at the supermarket.

NUTRITION (PER SERVE)

CALS	FAT	SAT FAT	PROTEIN	CARBS
330	11.1g	4.9g	32.7g	23g

Secret Hack

Time saver! If your slow cooker has a separate bowl, use that instead of a frying pan to save on time (and washing up).

● FREEZABLE   ○ GLUTEN FREE   ● MAKE AHEAD   ○ ONE POT   ○ VEGAN   ○ VEGO   ○ YEAR-ROUND FAVE

★★★★★

This is the most amazing slow-cooker beef recipe ever. No lie. This is THE recipe for beef. The sauce is super tasty but light, the flavours are well balanced and the meat is beautifully cooked. **POKIEDOT**

SPICE-RUBBED TURKEY

Use the slow cooker with aromatic spices for the star of the show and serve with deliciously crunchy potatoes.

SERVES 8 **PREP** 15 mins **COOK** 6 hours 25 mins

1 tbs sweet paprika
1 tbs brown sugar
2 tsp ground cumin
1 tsp fennel seeds
1 tsp garlic powder
1 tsp onion salt
1.5kg fresh single turkey breast
   with skin
1kg small baby white potatoes
685ml (2¾ cups) chicken stock
50g butter
35g (¼ cup) plain flour
1 tsp fresh thyme leaves
1 tbs chopped fresh continental
   parsley leaves

1 Combine paprika, sugar, cumin, fennel seeds, garlic powder and onion salt in a bowl. Rub mixture all over turkey. Season with pepper.

2 Place potatoes in base of slow cooker. Pour in 185ml (¾ cup) stock. Top with turkey. Cover. Cook on Low for 6 hours or until juices run clear when thickest part of turkey is pierced with a skewer.

3 Preheat oven to 240°C/220°C fan forced. Line a large baking tray with baking paper. Transfer turkey to a plate. Cover loosely with foil to keep warm. Set aside to rest, reserving 125ml (½ cup) cooking liquid.

4 Using a slotted spoon, transfer the potatoes to the prepared tray. Cut in half. Roast potatoes, turning, for 20-25 minutes or until golden and crisp.

5 Meanwhile, melt butter in a large frying pan. Add flour. Cook, stirring, until mixture turns golden. Gradually whisk in reserved liquid. Add remaining stock and thyme. Cook, whisking constantly, until mixture bubbles and thickens.

6 Slice turkey and serve with potatoes and gravy, scattered with parsley.

COOK'S NOTE

Steamed buttered peas are a delicious accompaniment for this meal.

NUTRITION (PER SERVE)

CALS	FAT	SAT FAT	PROTEIN	CARBS
463	22g	8g	43g	22g

○ FREEZABLE   ○ GLUTEN FREE   ● MAKE AHEAD   ○ ONE POT   ○ VEGAN   ○ VEGO   ○ YEAR-ROUND FAVE

PULLED PORK WITH
CHILLI

The chilli in this super-simple recipe gives the pork
an added kick without overwhelming the other flavours.

SERVES 8 **PREP** 5 mins **COOK** 8 hours

1.8kg boneless pork shoulder
2 tsp smoked paprika
1 small red onion, finely chopped
185ml (¾ cup) tomato sauce
2 tbs brown sugar
1½ tbs hot chilli sauce
1 tbs apple cider vinegar
1 tsp dried chilli flakes
Pork rind, for crackling

1 Place the pork in the base of the slow cooker. Rub with the paprika and season. Scatter the onion around the pork.

2 Combine the tomato sauce, sugar, chilli sauce, vinegar and chilli flakes in a bowl. Pour around the pork. Cover and cook on Low for 8 hours, turning halfway, or until the meat is very tender. Transfer the pork to a large bowl. Use two forks to coarsely shred the meat. Add enough of the cooking sauce to lightly coat the pork.

3 Meanwhile, for the crackling, preheat the oven to 220°C/200°C fan forced. Place pork rind on a tray and sprinkle generously with salt. Roast for 40 minutes or until the rind is crackled. Cut into pieces. Serve the pork with the remaining sauce and crackling.

COOK'S NOTE

If you don't want to put the oven on at all, skip the crackling. Serve pork on bread rolls with your favourite coleslaw.

NUTRITION (PER SERVE)

CALS	FAT	SAT FAT	PROTEIN	CARBS
649	47g	18g	45g	11g

○ FREEZABLE   ○ GLUTEN FREE   ● MAKE AHEAD   ○ ONE POT   ○ VEGAN   ○ VEGO   ● YEAR-ROUND FAVE

Secret Hack

For crispy crackling, dry thoroughly with a paper towel beforehand. You want the rind to be as dry as possible before adding salt.

CHICKEN WITH PESTO BUTTER

This classic flavour combination is always a winner and the slow cooker makes it super easy too.

SERVES 4 **PREP** 10 mins **COOK** 4 hours 10 mins

1.6kg whole chicken
60g butter, softened
2 tbs basil, cashew and parmesan dip
2 tbs chopped fresh basil leaves, plus extra leaves, to serve
1 garlic clove, finely chopped
1 tbs olive oil
Steamed carrots, beans and broccoli, to serve

1 Rinse chicken (including cavity) under cold running water. Pat dry with paper towel. Using your fingers, gently lift skin away from breast meat on each side to form 2 pockets.

2 Combine butter, dip, basil and garlic in a bowl. Gently push butter mixture under chicken skin, being careful not to split the skin.

3 Heat the oil in a large non-stick frying pan over medium heat. Add chicken, breast-side down. Cook, turning, for 10 minutes, or until golden. Place a wire rack in the base of the slow cooker. Place chicken on wire rack, breast-side up. Season. Cover and cook on Low for 4 hours or until chicken is tender and cooked through. Serve chicken with steamed vegetables and extra basil leaves.

COOK'S NOTE

If you don't have a wire rack that fits in your slow cooker, use roughly scrunched foil to lift the chicken from the base.

NUTRITION (PER SERVE)

CALS	FAT	SAT FAT	PROTEIN	CARBS
647	50g	18g	41g	6g

★★★★★ *My whole family enjoyed this chicken recipe... which is a rare occasion! I love the fresh basil butter taste!* **RACH1807**

○ FREEZABLE   ○ GLUTEN FREE   ● MAKE AHEAD   ○ ONE POT   ○ VEGAN   ○ VEGO   ● YEAR-ROUND FAVE

BEEF AND GUINNESS

BRISKET

The Guinness adds a depth of flavour to this rich and satisfying slow-cooked beef, served with classic buttered beans.

SERVES 8 **PREP** 20 mins **COOK** 8 hours 15 mins

2 tbs extra virgin olive oil
1.5kg piece beef brisket
1 leek, trimmed, halved, chopped
2 carrots, diced
3 hickory-smoked middle bacon
   rashers, trimmed, finely chopped
70g (¼ cup) tomato paste
3 sprigs fresh thyme
2 garlic cloves, crushed
2 dried bay leaves
375ml bottle Guinness
250ml (1 cup) beef stock

BUTTERED BEANS
50g butter
2 small red chillies, finely chopped
400g green beans, trimmed
¼ cup chopped fresh continental
   parsley leaves
1 tbs chopped fresh dill

1 Heat 1 tbs oil in a large heavy-based frying pan over medium-high heat. Cook beef for 5 minutes on each side or until browned. Transfer to the slow cooker.

2 Heat remaining oil in the same pan over medium heat. Add the leek, carrot and bacon. Cook, stirring occasionally, for 10 minutes or until leek has softened. Add tomato paste, thyme, garlic and bay leaves. Cook, stirring, for 1 minute or until fragrant. Stir in Guinness and stock. Season with pepper and bring to the boil.

3 Pour mixture over beef in the slow cooker. Cover and cook on Low for 8 hours. Remove and discard thyme and bay leaves. Coarsely shred beef.

4 Meanwhile, to make buttered beans, melt butter in a large frying pan over medium-high heat. Add chilli. Cook, stirring, for 30 seconds. Add beans. Cook, tossing, for 5 minutes or until beans are bright green and just tender. Remove from heat. Add parsley and dill. Season. Toss to coat. Serve brisket with buttered beans.

NUTRITION (PER SERVE)

CALS	FAT	SAT FAT	PROTEIN	CARBS
433	22g	9g	45g	7g

● FREEZABLE ○ GLUTEN FREE ● MAKE AHEAD ○ ONE POT ○ VEGAN ○ VEGO ○ YEAR-ROUND FAVE

★ ★ ★ ★ ★

This is the first slow-cooked meal I've ever made and it turned out perfect. **PORTIACOOK**

GREEK PORK WITH CHICKPEAS

Mediterranean flavours are the point of difference in this deliciously moist and simple meal.

SERVES 6 **PREP** 20 mins **COOK** 5 hours 10 mins

1 tsp cumin seeds
1 tsp fennel seeds
1 tsp dried oregano leaves
1½ tbs olive oil
1.2kg piece pork scotch fillet
1 red onion, coarsely chopped
2 garlic cloves, finely chopped
250ml (1 cup) passata
250ml (1 cup) chicken stock
1 tbs red wine vinegar
2 dried bay leaves
½ cinnamon stick
400g can chickpeas, rinsed, drained
⅓ cup chopped fresh coriander
Steamed rice and Greek-style
   yoghurt, to serve

1 Place cumin seeds, fennel seeds and oregano in a mortar and pound with a pestle until coarsely ground. Add 2 tsp of the oil and grind to form a paste. Rub over the pork. Season.

2 Heat the remaining oil in a large heavy-based frying pan over medium-high heat. Cook the pork, turning, for 5 minutes or until golden. Transfer to the slow cooker.

3 Add the onion and garlic to the frying pan and cook, stirring, for 3 minutes or until soft. Stir in passata, stock, vinegar, bay leaves and cinnamon. Add to the slow cooker with pork. Cover and cook for 5 hours on High until tender.

4 Stir in the chickpeas and coriander. Season with salt and pepper.

5 To thicken the sauce, if desired, transfer the pork to a plate and cover with foil to keep warm. Cook the sauce in the slow cooker, uncovered, for a further 30 minutes. Carve the pork. Serve with rice and yoghurt.

COOK'S NOTE

To make this recipe gluten free, make sure you use gluten-free stock and passata.

NUTRITION (PER SERVE)

CALS	FAT	SAT FAT	PROTEIN	CARBS
836	39g	14g	48g	70g

★★★★★ *So, so, so beautiful. Flavours perfectly balance and the meat was perfect. Cannot recommend enough.* **SHANWAAH**

○ FREEZABLE ● GLUTEN FREE ● MAKE AHEAD ○ ONE POT ○ VEGAN ○ VEGO ● YEAR-ROUND FAVE

INDIAN-STYLE BEEF ROAST

This roast beef has an Indian twist. Accompanied by pickled cucumber rice, it has a lovely aroma and fresh flavours.

SERVES 6 **PREP** 20 mins (+ chilling) **COOK** 8 hours 10 mins

1.5kg beef blade roast
2 tbs rogan josh curry paste
250ml (1 cup) beef stock
1 cinnamon stick
2 sprigs fresh curry leaves
Plain yoghurt and warmed naan bread, to serve

PICKLED CUCUMBER RICE

3 tsp vegetable oil
3 brown onions, halved, thinly sliced
2 tsp yellow mustard seeds
5 fresh curry leaves
3cm piece fresh ginger, grated
2 garlic cloves, crushed
400g (2 cups) basmati rice
750ml (3 cups) chicken stock
2 Lebanese cucumbers, peeled into ribbons
60ml (¼ cup) white vinegar
⅓ cup coarsely chopped fresh mint leaves

1. Place beef on a plate. Rub all over with curry paste. Place in the slow cooker. Add stock, cinnamon and curry leaves. Cover. Cook on Low for 8 hours (or High for 4 hours), turning halfway, or until beef is tender and cooked through.

2. Meanwhile, for the pickled cucumber rice, heat oil in a large heavy-based saucepan over medium-high heat. Add onion. Cook, stirring occasionally, for 8-10 minutes or until browned and tender. Add mustard seeds, curry leaves, ginger and garlic. Cook, stirring, for 1 minute or until seeds start to pop. Transfer mixture to a bowl. Set aside.

3. Place rice and stock in same pan over high heat. Stir to combine. Bring to the boil. Cover. Reduce heat to low. Simmer for 15-18 minutes or until liquid is absorbed and rice is tender. Fluff rice with a fork. Set aside for 10 minutes. Transfer to a bowl. Cover. Refrigerate for 1 hour.

4. Meanwhile, place cucumber and vinegar in a bowl. Season. Toss to combine. Cover. Chill in the fridge for 1 hour.

5. Drain cucumber. Add to rice with mint and half the onion mixture. Toss to combine. Spoon into a serving bowl. Top with remaining onion mixture.

6. Remove beef from cooking liquid. Transfer to a plate and cover to keep warm. Place cooking liquid in a small saucepan over medium-high heat. Bring to the boil. Reduce heat to low. Simmer for 10 minutes or until thickened slightly. Slice beef. Drizzle with cooking liquid. Serve with rice, yoghurt and naan bread.

NUTRITION (PER SERVE)

CALS	FAT	SAT FAT	PROTEIN	CARBS
973	21g	7g	70g	122g

○ FREEZABLE   ○ GLUTEN FREE   ● MAKE AHEAD   ○ ONE POT   ○ VEGAN   ○ VEGO   ● YEAR-ROUND FAVE

MIDDLE EASTERN LAMB WITH HUMMUS

This tender spiced lamb makes for a filling and warming meal, either just for the family, or to share with friends.

SERVES 4 **PREP** 20 mins **COOK** 6 hours

1.8kg leg of lamb, excess fat
    removed, scored
1 tbs Moroccan spice mix
1 tbs honey
Fresh mint and continental parsley
    leaves, to serve
Pine nuts, toasted, to serve
Lemon wedges, to serve
HUMMUS
400g can chickpeas, rinsed, drained
2 garlic cloves, chopped
½ tsp salt
125ml (½ cup) extra virgin olive oil
125ml (½ cup) tahini
2-3 tbs fresh lemon juice
125ml (½ cup) warm water

1 For the hummus, process the chickpeas, garlic and salt in a food processor until coarsely chopped. Add the oil and tahini. Add the lemon juice, to taste. With the motor running slowly add the water until the hummus reaches desired thickness. Transfer to a bowl. Cover and place in the fridge until required to develop the flavours.

2 Place the lamb in the bowl of a slow cooker. Season. Sprinkle over the spice mix and rub into the lamb. Drizzle with honey. Cook on High for 6 hours or until the lamb is very tender. Transfer the lamb to a chopping board and set aside for 10 minutes to rest. Shred the lamb meat and discard the bone. Spread the hummus over a large serving plate and top with the lamb. Scatter with mint, parsley and pine nuts and serve with lemon.

COOK'S NOTE

This would be great served with flatbread to mop up the hummus.

NUTRITION (PER SERVE)

CALS	FAT	SAT FAT	PROTEIN	CARBS
522	26g	8g	59g	11g

○ FREEZABLE   ○ GLUTEN FREE   ● MAKE AHEAD   ● ONE POT   ○ VEGAN   ○ VEGO   ● YEAR-ROUND FAVE

★★★★★ *This was ridiculously easy and tasted great. I used 1.5 tablespoons of Moroccan spice mix as my lamb leg was 2.4kg. Will make again for sure.* **KITCHENQUEEN**

20 mins prep

CORNED BEEF WITH

CIDER

This family favourite gets a modern update with a touch of apple cider and an accompanying salad of roasted apple and cabbage.

SERVES 8   **PREP** 20 mins   **COOK** 8 hours

2kg piece uncooked corned beef
1 brown onion, quartered
1 bunch baby carrots, trimmed
750g small baby white potatoes
500ml (2 cups) apple cider
2 tbs cider vinegar
2 dried bay leaves
1 tsp whole black peppercorns
Fresh dill sprigs, to serve

FENNEL-ROASTED APPLE AND CABBAGE

4 pink lady apples, quartered
½ small red cabbage, cut into small wedges
1 tsp fennel seeds
60ml (¼ cup) maple syrup, plus extra to serve
1 tbs extra virgin olive oil

1 Place corned beef, onion, carrots and potatoes in the slow cooker. Add cider, 125ml (½ cup) water, vinegar, bay leaves and peppercorns. Cover and cook on Low for 8 hours (or High for 4 hours), turning corned beef and vegetables halfway through cooking.

2 Meanwhile, to make the fennel-roasted apple and cabbage, preheat the oven to 200°C/180°C fan forced. Place the apple and cabbage in a roasting pan. Sprinkle with fennel seeds. Drizzle with the maple syrup and oil. Season. Roast, turning the apple and cabbage halfway through cooking, for 20-25 minutes or until just tender.

3 Remove corned beef from the slow cooker. Transfer to a board. Slice thickly. Drizzle apple mixture with a little extra maple syrup. Serve corned beef with roasted apple mixture, potatoes, carrots and a little cooking liquid, sprinkled with dill sprigs.

COOK'S NOTE

If you are a traditionalist, whip up your favourite white sauce and stir in some chopped parsley, to serve over the corned beef.

NUTRITION (PER SERVE)

CALS	FAT	SAT FAT	PROTEIN	CARBS
536	23g	5g	40g	36g

○ FREEZABLE   ○ GLUTEN FREE   ● MAKE AHEAD   ○ ONE POT   ○ VEGAN   ○ VEGO   ○ YEAR-ROUND FAVE

20 mins prep

33

LAMB RAAN WITH MINTED RICE

This slowly-does-it Indian favourite becomes a lot more achieveable with a slow cooker, allowing the flavours to develop beautifully.

SERVES 6 **PREP** 20 mins (+ 10 mins standing) **COOK** 8 hours 15 mins

130g (½ cup) plain Greek-style yoghurt, plus extra 200g (¾ cup), to serve
1 tsp ground turmeric
2 tbs ground cumin
2 tsp cracked black pepper
1 tsp salt
2 garlic cloves, crushed
1 tbs fresh lemon juice
2 tbs garam masala
2 tsp dried chilli flakes
1.5kg easy-carve leg of lamb
1 cinnamon stick
5 slices fresh ginger
1 bunch English spinach, steamed
Lemon wedges, to serve

MINTED RICE
300g (1½ cups) basmati rice, rinsed
Large pinch of saffron threads
⅓ cup chopped fresh mint leaves
35g (⅓ cup) flaked almonds, toasted

1 Combine yoghurt, turmeric, cumin, pepper, salt, garlic, juice, garam masala and chilli in a bowl. Cover lamb with mixture.

2 Place cinnamon stick and ginger in slow cooker. Add 250ml (1 cup) water. Top with lamb. Cover and cook on Low for 8 hours (or High for 4 hours) or until lamb is tender. Remove lid. Cook for a further 15 minutes.

3 Meanwhile, for the minted rice, place rice and saffron in a saucepan. Add 560ml (2¼ cups) water. Bring to the boil. Cover. Reduce heat to low. Simmer for 10 minutes or until liquid is absorbed. Remove from heat. Fluff with a fork. Cover. Stand for 10 minutes. Add mint and almonds. Season. Toss to combine. Serve lamb with rice, extra yoghurt, spinach and lemon wedges.

COOK'S NOTE

A tomato salad makes a great accompaniment to this dish.

NUTRITION (PER SERVE)

CALS	FAT	SAT FAT	PROTEIN	CARBS
611	24g	9g	50g	47g

○ FREEZABLE ● GLUTEN FREE ● MAKE AHEAD ○ ONE POT ○ VEGAN ○ VEGO ● YEAR-ROUND FAVE

LAMB WITH BEETROOT HUMMUS

Served with a colourful and tangy beetroot hummus, this delicious Persian-style casserole looks as good as it tastes.

SERVES 4 **PREP** 20 mins **COOK** 6 hours 10 mins

1 tbs extra virgin olive oil
3 brown onions, halved, sliced
4 garlic cloves, thinly sliced
125ml (½ cup) orange juice
1 dried bay leaf
1 tsp ground cumin
1 tsp ground cardamom
1 tsp ground cinnamon
2cm piece fresh ginger, peeled, finely grated
2 tsp finely grated orange rind, plus extra zest to serve
2 tbs pomegranate molasses
1.3kg half leg of lamb
½ cup fresh mint leaves
Arils of 1 pomegranate
220g tub sweet beetroot hummus
130g (½ cup) plain Greek-style yoghurt
4 Lebanese bread rounds

1 Heat the oil in a non-stick frying pan over medium-high heat. Cook onion for 5 minutes or until soft. Add garlic. Cook for 1 minute. Transfer to the slow cooker. Add orange juice and bay leaf. Season.

2 Combine ground spices, ginger, orange rind and molasses in a bowl. Season. Rub mixture all over lamb. Place lamb on top of onion mixture. Cover with lid. Cook on Low for 6 hours or until very tender.

3 Transfer lamb and sauce to a serving platter. Sprinkle with mint, pomegranate arils and extra orange zest. Serve with beetroot hummus, yoghurt and bread.

COOK'S NOTE

Serve with steamed rice instead of bread, if you prefer.

NUTRITION (PER SERVE)

CALS	FAT	SAT FAT	PROTEIN	CARBS
1052	50g	17g	65g	80g

★★★★★ *Amazing; fave dish right now.* **THEA MEAKER**

○ FREEZABLE ○ GLUTEN FREE ● MAKE AHEAD ○ ONE POT ○ VEGAN ○ VEGO ● YEAR-ROUND FAVE

CLASSIC ROAST BEEF AND VEGIES

This slow-cooker beef and vegies recipe has all the perfect ingredients for a Sunday roast. Make sure you have something to mop up the juices!

SERVES 6   **PREP** 15 mins   **COOK** 6 hours 25 mins

2 tbs extra virgin olive oil

1.8kg piece beef topside or beef blade roast

3 small pickling onions, quartered

2 garlic cloves, crushed

80ml (⅓ cup) dry white wine

3 tsp wholegrain mustard

375ml (1½ cups) beef stock

500g chat potatoes

1 bunch baby carrots, trimmed, peeled

3 sprigs fresh thyme

80g (½ cup) frozen peas

1 Heat half the oil in a large frying pan over medium-high heat. Cook beef for 6 minutes, turning, or until browned all over. Transfer to the slow cooker.

2 Heat remaining oil in pan. Add onion and garlic. Cook, stirring, for 3 minutes or until just softened. Add the wine. Reduce liquid by half. Stir in mustard and stock. Carefully transfer to the slow cooker.

3 Add the potatoes, carrot and thyme sprigs. Season with pepper. Cover and cook on Low for 6 hours or until the beef is tender.

4 Add the peas. Cook for 10 minutes. Serve sliced beef with vegetables, drizzled with a little cooking liquid or gravy (see note).

COOK'S NOTE

Serve with gravy if you prefer a thick sauce. Add 1 tbs cornflour to pan juices and stir over medium heat until thickened.

NUTRITION (PER SERVE)

CALS	FAT	SAT FAT	PROTEIN	CARBS
528	19g	6g	69g	16g

★★★★★

I had a piece of topside that worked well and was very tender. The sauce was rich and tasty from the slow cooker juices, which I added to, making a gravy with a packet of gravy mix. **WJLEITCH**

○ FREEZABLE   ○ GLUTEN FREE   ● MAKE AHEAD   ○ ONE POT   ○ VEGAN   ○ VEGO   ○ YEAR-ROUND FAVE

15
mins prep

HONEYED APRICOT LAMB WITH COUSCOUS

Served with an almond couscous, this delicious falling-apart fruity lamb dish is a total crowd-pleaser.

SERVES 4 **PREP** 15 mins **COOK** 6 hours 10 mins

2 tbs olive oil
800g lamb leg roast (boneless)
1 brown onion, thinly sliced
2 carrots, halved, cut into
  1cm thick slices
2 tsp Middle Eastern seasoning
2 garlic cloves, crushed
3 strips lemon rind
85g (½ cup) dried apricots
375ml (1½ cups) chicken stock
1 tbs honey
Steamed green beans, to serve

ALMOND COUSCOUS
290g (1½ cups) couscous
375ml (1½ cups) boiling water
½ cup flaked almonds, toasted
3 green shallots, thinly sliced

1 Heat half the oil in a large frying pan over medium-high heat. Cook lamb for 5 minutes, turning, until browned all over. Transfer to the slow cooker.

2 Heat remaining oil in the same pan. Add the onion and carrot. Cook, stirring, for 3 minutes. Add seasoning and garlic. Cook, stirring, for 1 minute or until fragrant. Transfer mixture to the slow cooker. Add the lemon rind, apricots, stock and honey. Season.

3 Cover and cook on Low for 6 hours or until lamb is tender, turning halfway during cooking. Transfer lamb leg to a plate. Remove and discard cooking string. Slice lamb. Spoon sauce over the top.

4 Meanwhile, to make the almond couscous, place couscous and boiling water in a heatproof bowl. Cover. Set aside for 5 minutes or until liquid is absorbed. Fluff with a fork to separate grains. Add almonds and shallots. Season. Toss to combine. Serve lamb with beans, almond couscous and apricot sauce.

COOK'S NOTE

We used a 5.5L slow cooker for this recipe.

NUTRITION (PER SERVE)

CALS	FAT	SAT FAT	PROTEIN	CARBS
802	29g	7g	56g	75g

○ FREEZABLE ○ GLUTEN FREE ● MAKE AHEAD ○ ONE POT ○ VEGAN ○ VEGO ○ YEAR-ROUND FAVE

NO-FUSS PORK WITH
LEMON SAGE

With just a few ingredients in your slow cooker you'll have a no-fuss pork roast for Sunday dinner.

SERVES 4 **PREP** 15 mins **COOK** 4 hours 15 mins

2 tbs olive oil
1 brown onion, finely chopped
1 garlic clove, crushed
2 tsp finely grated lemon rind
1 tbs finely chopped fresh
    sage leaves
105g (1½ cups) fresh breadcrumbs
    (see note)
1 egg, lightly beaten
1kg pork neck (scotch fillet)
Mashed potato, lemon wedges and
    sage leaves, to serve

1 Heat half the oil in a frying pan over medium-high heat. Cook onion and garlic for 3-4 minutes or until onion has softened. Place onion mixture in a bowl. Add lemon rind, sage, breadcrumbs and egg. Stir to combine. Season.

2 Place pork on a chopping board. Cut lengthways without cutting all the way through. Open pork out. Press on stuffing. Fold pork over to enclose stuffing. Tie with kitchen string at 3cm intervals to secure.

3 Heat remaining oil in a large frying pan on medium-high heat. Add pork. Cook, turning, for 8 minutes or until pork is browned. Transfer to the slow cooker. Cover. Cook on High for 4 hours or until tender and cooked through. Slice. Serve with mash, lemon wedges and sage leaves.

COOK'S NOTE

Use gluten-free breadcrumbs for the stuffing to make this recipe gluten free.

NUTRITION (PER SERVE)

CALS	FAT	SAT FAT	PROTEIN	CARBS
451	16g	4g	61g	16g

○ FREEZABLE ○ GLUTEN FREE ● MAKE AHEAD ○ ONE POT ○ VEGAN ○ VEGO ● YEAR-ROUND FAVE

★ ★ ★ ★ ★

Very tender and tasty, and super easy.
Had it for a celebration dinner one night and leftovers
with kids next night. Big success both nights. **DAMEDEL**

15 mins prep

43

LAMB CHOPS IN RED WINE

This budget-friendly dish with minimal prep time has a French-inspired sauce to take it above the ordinary.

SERVES 4 **PREP** 20 mins **COOK** 5 hours 10 mins

1 tsp olive oil
1kg lamb forequarter chops, trimmed
1 red onion, halved, thinly sliced
3 garlic cloves, thinly sliced
400g can finely chopped tomatoes
2 tbs tomato paste
250ml (1 cup) dry red wine (see note)
5 sprigs fresh thyme
1 sprig fresh rosemary
305g (1½ cups) risoni
100g reduced-fat feta, crumbled
⅓ cup chopped continental
   parsley leaves
2 tsp shredded lemon rind

1 Heat the oil in large deep non-stick frying pan over medium-high heat. Season lamb chops. Add half the lamb to pan. Cook for 2-3 minutes each side or until browned. Transfer to the slow cooker. Repeat with the remaining lamb.

2 Reduce heat to medium. Add onion. Cook, stirring often, for 5 minutes or until softened. Add garlic. Cook for 1 minute or until fragrant. Add tomato, paste, wine, thyme and rosemary. Season. Pour over the lamb. Cover and cook on Low for 5 hours or until lamb is tender.

3 Cook pasta in a large saucepan of boiling, salted water, following packet directions, until tender. Drain.

4 Sprinkle lamb with feta, parsley and lemon rind. Serve with risoni.

COOK'S NOTE

You can replace the red wine with beef stock, if preferred.

NUTRITION (PER SERVE)

CALS	FAT	SAT FAT	PROTEIN	CARBS
691	22g	8g	46g	64g

● FREEZABLE ○ GLUTEN FREE ● MAKE AHEAD ○ ONE POT ○ VEGAN ○ VEGO ● YEAR-ROUND FAVE

★★★★★
Cooked according to recipe
and it was absolutely delicious.
Served with mashed potato and peas.
Will be keeping this as a favourite.
A definite winner. GABRIELE65OGS

20
mins prep

ROAST BEEF WITH
HORSERADISH

A classical tender dish with horseradish for zing and heat.
Serve with traditional vegies for the complete experience.

SERVES 6 **PREP** 10 mins **COOK** 6 hours 10 mins

1.2kg beef bolar blade roast,
   excess fat removed
6 golden delight potatoes,
   peeled, quartered
4 carrots, halved lengthways
1 tbs olive oil
¼ cup chopped fresh continental
   parsley leaves
⅓ cup instant roast meat
   gravy powder
Horseradish cream and extra
   chopped parsley, to serve

1 Using kitchen string, tie up beef at 4cm intervals to secure. Place potato and carrot in the slow cooker. Heat oil in a large frying pan. Cook beef, turning, for 5 minutes or until browned all over. Place on vegetables in the slow cooker.

2 Add 180ml (¾ cup) cold water. Sprinkle with parsley. Season. Cover and cook on Low for 6 hours (or on High for 3 hours).

3 Transfer beef and vegetables to a large plate. Thickly slice carrots. Cover loosely with foil to keep warm. Sprinkle the gravy powder into the sauce in the slow cooker. Whisk well to combine. Cook, whisking often, for 5 minutes or until gravy thickens.

4 Slice beef. Serve with vegetables, gravy and horseradish cream, topped with extra parsley.

COOK'S NOTE

Try serving with crusty bread to mop up the delicious gravy.

NUTRITION (PER SERVE)

CALS	FAT	SAT FAT	PROTEIN	CARBS
427	12g	5g	44g	31g

○ FREEZABLE ○ GLUTEN FREE ● MAKE AHEAD ○ ONE POT ○ VEGAN ○ VEGO ○ YEAR-ROUND FAVE

★ ★ ★ ★ ★

This dish was delicious. I put it in my auto slow cooker for 4 hours and then left it keeping warm for another hour or so. When it came out it was a 'pull' consistency. With the gravy and horseradish sauce, excellent dish. **SHGREGSON**

10 *mins prep*

47

PORK WITH SAGE AND APPLE

Enjoy the ease of using a slow cooker, without sacrificing the traditional crackling and apple sauce.

SERVES 8 **PREP** 20 mins **COOK** 8 hours 10 mins

2kg pork shoulder, rind removed and reserved
2 tbs olive oil
4 French shallots, thinly sliced
¼ cup coarsely chopped fresh sage leaves, plus extra leaves to serve
4 garlic cloves, crushed
2 fresh thyme sprigs
4 fresh bay leaves
330ml btl crushed apple cider
160ml (⅔ cup) chicken stock
2 tbs maple syrup
4 Granny Smith apples, peeled, cored, chopped
1 tbs caster sugar
2 tsp white wine vinegar

1 Remove and discard excess fat from reserved rind. Score rind at 2.5cm intervals. Place rind, skin-side up, on a wire rack set over a baking tray. Refrigerate until needed. Tie up pork with kitchen string at 5cm intervals.

2 Heat half the oil in a large frying pan over medium-high heat. Add pork. Cook, turning, for 5 minutes or until browned. Transfer to the slow cooker.

3 Reduce heat to medium. Heat half the remaining oil in the same pan. Add shallot. Cook for 4 minutes or until softened. Add sage and garlic. Cook for 1 minute or until fragrant. Transfer to slow cooker. Add thyme sprigs and bay leaves. Combine cider, stock and maple syrup in a jug and add to the slow cooker. Cover and cook on Low for 6-8 hours (or on High for 4 hours), adding the apple halfway through cooking time.

4 Meanwhile, preheat the oven to 220°C/200°C fan forced. Rub rind with remaining oil. Sprinkle with salt. Roast for 40-50 minutes until golden and crisp. Set aside to cool, then cut into strips.

5 Transfer pork to a plate and cover with foil to keep warm. Transfer apple and 60ml (¼ cup) cooking liquid to a food processor. Add sugar and vinegar. Process until chopped.

6 Remove and discard string from pork. Slice. Finely chop some of the extra sage leaves and sprinkle over the pork. Serve with crackling and apple sauce on the side and scatter some whole sage leaves over.

NUTRITION (PER SERVE)

CALS	FAT	SAT FAT	PROTEIN	CARBS
575	33g	13g	47g	20g

○ FREEZABLE　○ GLUTEN FREE　● MAKE AHEAD　○ ONE POT　○ VEGAN　○ VEGO　○ YEAR-ROUND FAVE

★★★★★

It was soooo good! It was an amazing dish to have for winter.
The smells were incredible, it reminded me of gluhwein, such rich spicy
smell from the herbs and cider. **SUEMCLEOD123**

SOUPS

HEARTY YET HEALTHY, AROMATIC AND NOURISHING,
SERVE ANY OF THESE SOUPS AS A MAIN MEAL.

VEGETABLE HARIRA

This aromatic, spice-laden Moroccan classic soup is given a healthy vego twist – which also makes it budget-friendly too.

SERVES 8 **PREP** 10 mins **COOK** 6 hours 10 mins

1 tbs extra virgin olive oil
3 garlic cloves, crushed
1 large brown onion, finely chopped
2 carrots, finely chopped
2 celery sticks, finely chopped
2 tsp ground cumin
2 tsp ground coriander
2 tsp mild paprika
1 tsp ground ginger
½ tsp ground cinnamon
½ tsp dried chilli flakes
2 tbs tomato paste
4 tomatoes, chopped
2L (8 cups) salt-reduced
   vegetable stock
130g (⅔ cup) dried green
   lentils, rinsed
100g (½ cup) basmati rice
400g can chickpeas, rinsed, drained
1½ cups frozen broad beans,
   thawed, peeled
½ cup chopped fresh
   coriander leaves
Plain reduced-fat Greek-style yoghurt
   and lemon wedges, to serve

1 Heat oil in a frying pan over medium heat. Cook garlic, onion, carrot and celery, stirring, for 5-7 minutes or until softened. Add spices. Cook, stirring, for 1 minute. Add tomato paste. Cook, stirring, for 1 minute.

2 Transfer mixture to the slow cooker. Stir in tomato, stock, lentils and 750ml (3 cups) water. Cook, covered, on Low for 6 hours, adding rice halfway through cooking time.

3 Stir chickpeas and beans into soup. Cover and continue cooking for 5 minutes. Season. Ladle among bowls. Top with coriander and yoghurt. Serve with lemon wedges.

COOK'S NOTE

Omit the yoghurt or substitute coconut yoghurt to make this recipe suitable for vegans.

NUTRITION (PER SERVE)

CALS	FAT	SAT FAT	PROTEIN	CARBS
257	5g	1g	12g	35g

● FREEZABLE ○ GLUTEN FREE ● MAKE AHEAD ○ ONE POT ○ VEGAN ● VEGO ● YEAR-ROUND FAVE

10
mins prep

CHICKPEA SOUP WITH LAMB

This low-cal and gluten-free soup works well for lunch or light meals and it also freezes well, so it's perfect for batch cooking.

SERVES 4 **PREP** 15 mins **COOK** 7 hours

2 tsp extra virgin olive oil
2 large French-trimmed lamb shanks
1 large brown onion, finely chopped
1 carrot, peeled, finely chopped
2 celery sticks, finely chopped
2 garlic cloves, crushed
2 tsp cumin seeds, crushed
2 tsp brown mustard seeds
2 tsp sweet paprika
1 tsp ground coriander
400g can chopped tomatoes
400g can chickpeas, rinsed, drained
500ml (2 cups) salt-reduced gluten-
    free chicken stock
100g trimmed silverbeet (about
    ½ bunch), chopped
Natural yoghurt, to serve (optional)

1 Heat half the oil in a large non-stick frying pan over high heat. Cook lamb for 1-2 minutes each side or until browned. Transfer to the slow cooker.

2 Heat remaining oil in the same pan over medium heat. Cook onion, carrot and celery, stirring, for 5 minutes or until soft. Add garlic, cumin, mustard, paprika and coriander. Cook, stirring, for 1 minute. Transfer vegie mixture to slow cooker. Stir in tomato, chickpeas, stock and 500ml (2 cups) water. Cover and cook on Low for 6 hours 30 minutes.

3 Transfer lamb to a bowl. Once cool enough to handle, shred meat and discard bones. Return meat to the slow cooker. Add silverbeet. Cover. Cook for a further 20 minutes. Season. Serve with yoghurt, if using.

COOK'S NOTE

You could use canned brown lentils, cannellini or borlotti beans in place of the chickpeas, if preferred.

NUTRITION (PER SERVE)

CALS	FAT	SAT FAT	PROTEIN	CARBS
268	11g	3g	24g	16g

★ ★ ★ ★ ★

*This is one of the best soups I have ever tasted!
So hearty and healthy.* **ALEXANDRA_BRAZI**

○ FREEZABLE ● GLUTEN FREE ● MAKE AHEAD ○ ONE POT ○ VEGAN ○ VEGO ○ YEAR-ROUND FAVE

VEGETARIAN MINESTRONE

Come home to a hearty vegie staple: with only 15 minutes of prep needed, this will be on high rotation during the winter months.

SERVES 6 **PREP** 15 mins **COOK** 6 hours 45 mins

2 tbs olive oil
1 red onion, finely chopped
3 celery sticks, finely chopped
3 carrots, peeled, finely chopped
1 fennel bulb, trimmed, core removed, finely chopped
3 garlic cloves, crushed
2.5L (10 cups) vegetable stock
400g can chopped tomatoes
400g can borlotti beans, rinsed, drained
1 parmesan rind (optional)
145g (1 cup) small dried macaroni
160g (4 cups) chopped purple kale leaves
Basil pesto, fresh purple basil leaves, finely grated parmesan and bread, to serve

1 Heat the oil in a large frying pan over medium-high heat. Add the onion, celery, carrot and fennel and cook, stirring regularly, for 10 minutes or until the vegetables are soft and lightly golden. Add garlic. Cook, stirring, for 1 minute or until aromatic. Transfer to the slow cooker. Stir in the stock, tomato, beans and parmesan rind, if using. Cover and cook on Low for 6 hours.

2 Add the macaroni to the slow cooker. Stir to combine. Cover. Cook for a further 30 minutes or until pasta is al dente. Discard the parmesan rind. Stir in half the kale.

3 Divide soup among serving bowls. Top with remaining kale and add a few dollops of pesto. Scatter with the basil and sprinkle with grated parmesan. Serve with bread.

COOK'S NOTE

Use a large (6L) slow cooker for this recipe, as the pasta will expand when cooked.

NUTRITION (PER SERVE)

CALS	FAT	SAT FAT	PROTEIN	CARBS
393	16g	3g	13g	46g

★★★★★

I used risoni pasta, but only added ¼ cup. Really nice soup! **KTFOOD**

● FREEZABLE ○ GLUTEN FREE ● MAKE AHEAD ○ ONE POT ○ VEGAN ● VEGO ○ YEAR-ROUND FAVE

15
mins prep

PEA AND HAM SOUP

This hearty winter soup has a delicious apple parsnip twist that'll keep everyone coming back for more.

SERVES 6 **PREP** 20 mins **COOK** 8 hours 10 mins

1 tbs extra virgin olive oil, plus extra, to drizzle
1 brown onion, coarsely chopped
2 tsp ground cumin
1kg smoked ham hock
4 parsnips, peeled, chopped
2 green apples, peeled, cored, coarsely chopped
530g (2½ cups) green split peas
1 large lemon, rind finely grated, plus extra zest, to serve
Crème fraîche and fresh mint, to serve

1 Heat the oil in a small frying pan over high heat. Add the onion and cook, stirring, for 5 minutes or until soft. Stir in the cumin and cook for 30 seconds or until aromatic. Transfer the mixture to the slow cooker.

2 Add the ham hock, parsnip, apple, split peas and 2L (8 cups) water to the slow cooker. Stir well. Cover. Cook on High for 6-8 hours or until ham is very tender.

3 Use tongs or a slotted spoon to transfer the ham hock to a chopping board. Use a stick blender to blend the soup until smooth, adding up to 250ml (1 cup) extra water if the mixture is too thick. Stir in the lemon rind.

4 Remove the ham from the hock, discarding the bone, skin and fat. Divide the soup among serving bowls. Top with crème fraîche, ham, mint and lemon zest. Drizzle with extra oil and season with pepper.

COOK'S NOTE

This soup will keep, covered, in the fridge for up to 3 days.

NUTRITION (PER SERVE)

CALS	FAT	SAT FAT	PROTEIN	CARBS
573	18g	6g	38g	55g

● FREEZABLE ● GLUTEN FREE ● MAKE AHEAD ○ ONE POT ○ VEGAN ○ VEGO ○ YEAR-ROUND FAVE

★★★★★ *I made this yesterday for the first time. Absolutely amazing! Even better for lunch today.* **OXY**

RED LENTIL BROTH

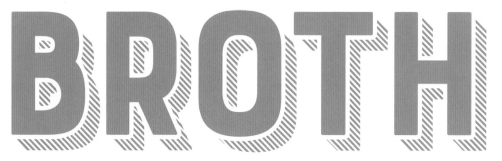

This hearty dish is perfect for lunch or an easy evening meal – with minimal prep and maximum taste, it's pretty well a set-and-forget recipe.

SERVES 6 **PREP** 10 mins **COOK** 4 hours 10 mins

2 tsp olive oil
1 brown onion, chopped
2 carrots, chopped
2 celery sticks, chopped
2 garlic cloves, thinly sliced
4cm piece fresh ginger, peeled, finely chopped
3 tsp ground cumin
3 tsp ground coriander
300g (1½ cups) red lentils
1L (4 cups) vegetable stock
Plain Greek-style yoghurt, fresh coriander leaves and warmed garlic naan bread, to serve

1 Heat oil in a large non-stick frying pan over medium heat. Add onion, carrot and celery. Cook, stirring often, for 5 minutes or until softened. Add garlic and ginger. Cook for 1 minute or until fragrant. Add cumin and coriander. Cook, stirring, for 30 seconds or until fragrant. Transfer to the slow cooker.

2 Add lentils, stock and 500ml (2 cups) cold water. Season. Cover with the lid. Cook on Low for 4 hours or until thickened.

3 Divide among serving bowls. Top with yoghurt and coriander. Serve with naan bread.

COOK'S NOTE

Omit the yoghurt to create a lovely vegan dish.

NUTRITION (PER SERVE)

CALS	FAT	SAT FAT	PROTEIN	CARBS
696	14g	3.4g	34g	98g

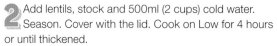

★★★★★

Made this exactly as the recipe stated and it was delicious. Served it with coriander, yoghurt and a squeeze of lime. **RSIDE**

● FREEZABLE ○ GLUTEN FREE ● MAKE AHEAD ○ ONE POT ○ VEGAN ● VEGO ● YEAR-ROUND FAVE

10
mins prep

FRENCH-STYLE SOUP WITH CHICKEN

This rustic chicken and vegetable soup has minimal prep and will fill your home with delicious smells while it's cooking.

SERVES 4 **PREP** 10 mins **COOK** 6 hours 5 mins

2 tsp extra virgin olive oil
6 (900g) chicken lovely legs
2 celery sticks, trimmed, thinly sliced
2 carrots, chopped
1 leek, trimmed, halved, thinly sliced
1 fennel bulb (fronds reserved), trimmed, chopped
1.25L (5 cups) salt-reduced chicken stock
3 fresh thyme sprigs
60g (½ cup) frozen peas
4 slices crusty bread, to serve

1 Heat oil in a non-stick frying pan over medium-high heat. Add chicken. Cook, turning, for 5 minutes or until browned all over. Transfer to the slow cooker.

2 Add celery, carrot, leek, fennel, stock and thyme. Season. Cover with lid. Cook on Low for 6 hours (or on High for 4 hours). Add peas in the last 10 minutes of cooking time. Remove and discard thyme.

3 Remove chicken from soup and transfer to a board. Remove and discard bones. Coarsely shred the chicken and return to soup.

4 Scatter with reserved fennel fronds and serve with crusty bread.

COOK'S NOTE

Chicken lovely legs are drumsticks that have had skin and fat removed, making them a healthier alternative.

NUTRITION (PER SERVE)

CALS	FAT	SAT FAT	PROTEIN	CARBS
606	12g	3g	54g	64g

★★★★★ *Love this soup, light yet filling. Have it for lunch everyday. Also freezes well.* **BETTYBOO0511**

● FREEZABLE ○ GLUTEN FREE ● MAKE AHEAD ○ ONE POT ○ VEGAN ○ VEGO ● YEAR-ROUND FAVE

SWEET POTATO SOUP WITH HARISSA

Served with spiced chickpeas for added crunch, this rich soup is full of Moroccan flavours, such as cumin, harissa and paprika.

SERVES 6 **PREP** 15 mins **COOK** 8 hours 10 mins

1 tbs extra virgin olive oil

1 tbs Moroccan spice mix

2 brown onions, finely chopped

3 large garlic cloves, crushed

285g jar roasted red peppers, rinsed, drained, halved

1-2 tsp harissa paste, to taste

2 large (about 800g) sweet potatoes, peeled, cut into 5cm pieces

3 large carrots, peeled, cut into 5cm pieces

1L (4 cups) vegetable stock

400g can chickpeas, rinsed, drained

1 tsp honey

Greek-style yoghurt, to serve

Baby coriander, to serve (optional)

SPICED CHICKPEAS

2 tsp extra virgin olive oil

400g can chickpeas, rinsed, drained, patted dry

2-3 tbs pepitas

½ tsp ground cumin

½ tsp smoked paprika

1 Heat the oil in a large frying pan over medium heat. Add spice mix. Cook, stirring, for 30 seconds or until aromatic. Add onion. Cook, stirring, for 3-4 minutes or until softened. Add garlic, peppers and harissa. Cook, stirring, for 2 minutes or until aromatic. Transfer to the slow cooker. Wipe frying pan clean with paper towel and set aside.

2 Add the sweet potato, carrot, stock, chickpeas and honey to the slow cooker. Season with pepper. Stir to combine. Cover with the lid. Set on Low and cook for 6-8 hours or until vegetables are tender. Blend until smooth. Stir in 250ml (1 cup) water if soup is too thick. Season.

3 Meanwhile, to make the spiced chickpeas, heat the oil in the frying pan over medium-high heat. Add chickpeas, pepitas, cumin and paprika. Cook, shaking the pan occasionally, for 6-10 minutes or until crisp. Season.

4 Divide soup among bowls. Top with yoghurt and chickpea mixture and scatter with coriander, if using.

COOK'S NOTE

To make this vegan, omit the yoghurt and sweeten with maple syrup instead of honey.

NUTRITION (PER SERVE)

CALS	FAT	SAT FAT	PROTEIN	CARBS
317	10g	2g	9g	41g

● FREEZABLE   ○ GLUTEN FREE   ● MAKE AHEAD   ○ ONE POT   ○ VEGAN   ● VEGO   ○ YEAR-ROUND FAVE

15
mins prep

★★★★★
*The soup was fine, but [the toppings]
really brought out all the flavours
nicely.* **BROOKELAUREN22**

SOUP WITH HAM AND LENTILS

With just 10 minutes of prep, this richly flavoured slow-cooker soup is the perfect winter warmer.

SERVES 4 **PREP** 10 mins **COOK** 8 hours 5 mins

2 carrots, thickly sliced
2 celery sticks, sliced
1 (850g) ham hock
1 brown onion, chopped
700g tomato passata
2 salt-reduced chicken stock cubes
200g (1 cup) dried brown lentils, rinsed, drained
3 fresh thyme sprigs, plus extra to serve
2 dried bay leaves
80g baby spinach
Crusty bread rolls, to serve

1 Place carrot, celery, ham hock, onion, passata, stock cubes, lentils, thyme, bay leaves and 1.25L (5 cups) water in the slow cooker. Cover with lid. Cook on Low for 8 hours (or on High for 4 hours) or until lentils have softened and ham hock is tender.

2 Transfer ham hock to a heatproof bowl. Remove and discard rind and bone. Using two forks, shred meat. Return ham to the slow cooker. Cook, covered, on High for 5 minutes. Stir in spinach. Turn off slow cooker and leave covered for 2 minutes, then season.

3 Ladle soup among serving bowls. Top with extra thyme. Serve with bread rolls.

COOK'S NOTE

Serve over cooked pasta for an even heartier meal.

NUTRITION (PER SERVE)

CALS	FAT	SAT FAT	PROTEIN	CARBS
501	13g	5g	38g	52g

★★★★★ *Very easy and so tasty. Will be making again.* **STICKEZ**

● FREEZABLE ○ GLUTEN FREE ● MAKE AHEAD ● ONE POT ○ VEGAN ○ VEGO ○ YEAR-ROUND FAVE

TUSCAN-STYLE RIBOLLITA

This famous rustic Italian bread soup is super easy and super healthy. Adding the bread at the last minute makes it hearty as well.

SERVES 4 **PREP** 10 mins **COOK** 4 hours 40 mins

2 tsp olive oil
1 brown onion, finely chopped
2 carrots, peeled, chopped
2 celery sticks, trimmed, chopped
2 garlic cloves, crushed
1 tsp fennel seeds
Pinch of dried chilli flakes
400g can crushed tomatoes
400g can cannellini beans, rinsed, drained
1L (4 cups) vegetable stock
Bouquet garni (4 fresh or dried bay leaves, 4 fresh sprigs thyme, 2 fresh sprigs rosemary)
200g cavolo nero (Tuscan cabbage), stem removed, leaves shredded
2 thick slices Italian bread (*pane di casa*), lightly toasted, torn into chunks
40g (½ cup) finely grated parmesan, plus extra shaved, to serve
1 lemon, juiced, rind zested
Continental parsley, to serve

1 Heat oil in a large non-stick frying pan over medium-high heat. Cook onion, carrot and celery for 5 minutes or until tender. Add the garlic, fennel and chilli. Cook for 1 minute. Transfer to the slow cooker. Add the tomato, beans, stock and bouquet garni. Season. Cover and cook on High for 3-4 hours or until vegetables are almost tender.

2 Stir in the cavolo nero, bread and parmesan. Cover and continue to cook on High for 30 minutes or until soup has thickened slightly. Stir in lemon juice, to taste. Serve topped with parsley, lemon zest and extra parmesan.

COOK'S NOTE

If your bread is slightly stale, don't worry about toasting it.

NUTRITION (PER SERVE)

CALS	FAT	SAT FAT	PROTEIN	CARBS
261	8g	3g	14g	26g

○ FREEZABLE   ○ GLUTEN FREE   ● MAKE AHEAD   ○ ONE POT   ○ VEGAN   ● VEGO   ○ YEAR-ROUND FAVE

★★★★★

I cooked this on the stove top and it was perfect. Lovely flavours and healthy. Used kale instead of Tuscan cabbage. **MOLLYFLANDERS**

10 *mins prep*

SPICY BLACK BEAN
BOWL

This bean and corn soup has a great chilli kick to complement its creamy consistency. The beans add protein and fibre to make it even healthier.

SERVES 4 **PREP** 15 mins **COOK** 8 hours 15 mins

220g (1 cup) dried black beans, rinsed, drained
2 tsp extra virgin olive oil
1 large brown onion, finely chopped
2 celery sticks, finely chopped
2 garlic cloves, crushed
2 tsp ground cumin
2 tsp sweet paprika
½ tsp dried chilli flakes
400g can crushed tomatoes
300g sweet potato, peeled, chopped
1 large corncob, kernels removed
2 tbs chopped fresh coriander leaves
1 fresh long green chilli, deseeded, finely chopped
Lime wedges, to serve

1 Place black beans in a large saucepan. Cover with enough cold water to come 5cm above beans. Bring to the boil over medium-high heat. Cook for 10 minutes. Drain well.

2 Meanwhile, heat oil in a large non-stick frying pan over medium heat. Cook onion and celery, stirring, for 5 minutes or until soft. Add garlic, cumin, paprika and chilli. Cook, stirring, for 1 minute or until aromatic.

3 Transfer the onion mixture and beans to the slow cooker and add the tomato and 1.25L (5 cups) water. Cover and cook on Low for 7 hours. Add the sweet potato and corn. Cover and cook for a further 1 hour or until sweet potato is tender and soup is thick. Season.

4 Combine coriander and green chilli in a small bowl. Divide soup among serving bowls. Top with coriander mixture. Serve with lime wedges for squeezing over.

COOK'S NOTE

A large (6L) slow cooker is recommended for this recipe.

NUTRITION (PER SERVE)

CALS	FAT	SAT FAT	PROTEIN	CARBS
346	14g	2g	21g	29g

● FREEZABLE ○ GLUTEN FREE ● MAKE AHEAD ○ ONE POT ● VEGAN ● VEGO ○ YEAR-ROUND FAVE

★★★★★ *This is a fantastic, nutritious soup. The lime, coriander and chilli make it burst with flavour. I make this for my non-vegan friends and family and they all love it too.* MAREE_K

LENTIL SOUP WITH CHEESE TOAST

The sharp flavour of goat's cheese toast is the perfect accompaniment to this hearty and rich lentil soup.

SERVES 4 **PREP** 10 mins **COOK** 3 hours

1 brown onion, finely chopped
2 celery sticks, trimmed,
   coarsely chopped
1 carrot, peeled, coarsely chopped
1 swede, peeled, coarsely chopped
1 garlic clove, crushed
115g (½ cup) red lentils
2 x 400g cans chopped tomatoes
500ml (2 cups) vegetable stock
3 tsp ground cumin
1 French bread stick (baguette),
   thinly sliced diagonally
100g goat's cheese
¼ cup chopped fresh chives

1 Place the onion, celery, carrot, swede, garlic, lentils, tomato, stock and cumin in the slow cooker. Cover and cook on High for 3 hours or until the vegetables are tender and the soup is thick.

2 Near the end of the cooking time, preheat the grill on high. Place the bread on a baking tray. Cook for 2 minutes each side or until golden. Combine the goat's cheese and chives in a small bowl. Spread the goat's cheese mixture over the toast.

3 Divide the soup among serving bowls and serve with the goat's cheese toast.

COOK'S NOTE

If you aren't a fan of goat's cheese, use a spreadable cream cheese for a milder flavour.

NUTRITION (PER SERVE)

CALS	FAT	SAT FAT	PROTEIN	CARBS
395g	11g	5g	20g	55g

● FREEZABLE   ○ GLUTEN FREE   ● MAKE AHEAD   ● ONE POT   ○ VEGAN   ● VEGO   ○ YEAR-ROUND FAVE

10 mins prep

★★★★★ I cooked this soup for a *LONG* time in my slow cooker – about 8 hours on low then another 3 on high. It was so delish even my soup-hating hubby ate a huge bowl of it. **TROON80**

73

MEXICAN CHICKEN SOUP WITH CORN

This delicious soup includes Mexican spices balanced with sour cream and crispy corn chips for added authenticity.

SERVES 4   **PREP** 15 mins   **COOK** 6 hours 45 mins

2 tsp olive oil
4 chicken thigh fillets, fat trimmed
1 brown onion, finely chopped
2 garlic cloves, crushed
1.5L (6 cups) chicken stock
3 tsp chipotle in adobo sauce
4 corncobs, husks and silk removed
400g can black beans, rinsed, drained
2 tbs fresh lime juice
85g (⅓ cup) sour cream
Hot chilli sauce, to drizzle
2 green shallots, thinly sliced
¼ cup fresh coriander
    leaves, chopped
Lime wedges and blue corn chips,
    to serve

1 Heat the oil in a large frying pan over medium heat. Add the chicken and cook for 3 minutes each side or until golden brown. Transfer to the slow cooker. Add the onion to the frying pan and cook, stirring, for 5 minutes or until soft and lightly golden. Add garlic and cook, stirring, for 30 seconds or until aromatic. Transfer to the slow cooker.

2 Add stock to the slow cooker, then stir in the chipotle. Add corncobs. Cover and cook on Low for 6 hours.

3 Use tongs to transfer the corncobs and chicken thighs to a chopping board. Set aside to cool slightly. Use a small sharp knife to cut the corn kernels from the cobs. Coarsely chop the chicken. Return corn kernels and chicken to the soup. Add the black beans and stir to combine. Cover and cook on High for 30 minutes or until the soup is heated through.

4 Stir in the lime juice. Ladle the soup into serving bowls and top with sour cream, chilli sauce, green shallot and coriander. Serve with lime wedges and corn chips.

COOK'S NOTE

Chipotle chillies are dried jalapeno chillies usually packed in adobo sauce. You will find them in jars or cans in the international section of the supermarket.

NUTRITION (PER SERVE)

CALS	FAT	SAT FAT	PROTEIN	CARBS
609	26g	10g	42g	43g

● FREEZABLE   ○ GLUTEN FREE   ● MAKE AHEAD   ○ ONE POT   ○ VEGAN   ○ VEGO   ● YEAR-ROUND FAVE

BEEF AND BARLEY SOUP

Low in fat and carbs, this super-healthy winter soup will fill you up – and makes a great lunch idea.

SERVES 4 **PREP** 15 mins **COOK** 7 hours 15 mins

2 tsp olive oil
500g beef blade steak, trimmed, chopped
2 carrots, peeled, finely chopped
2 celery sticks, trimmed, chopped
1 large brown onion, finely chopped
2 garlic cloves, crushed
2 tsp fresh thyme leaves
500ml (2 cups) salt-reduced beef stock
400g can chopped tomatoes
75g (⅓ cup) pearl barley, rinsed, drained
100g trimmed cavolo nero (Tuscan cabbage), shredded
Chopped fresh continental parsley, to serve
Baby herb sprigs, to serve

1 Heat half the oil in a large non-stick frying pan over high heat. Cook the beef in batches, stirring, for 2-3 minutes or until well browned. Transfer to the slow cooker.

2 Heat the remaining oil in the pan over medium heat. Add the carrot, celery and onion. Cook, stirring, for 5-6 minutes or until soft. Add the garlic and thyme. Cook, stirring, for 1 minute or until aromatic.

3 Add the stock, 375ml (1½ cups) water, tomato and pearl barley. Bring to the boil, then carefully pour into the slow cooker with the beef. Cover and cook on Low for 6 hours or until beef is tender. Add the cavolo nero, cover and cook for a further 1 hour or until tender. Season with pepper to taste. Scatter with the parsley and herb sprigs to serve.

COOK'S NOTE

If you can't find cavolo nero, use kale or even just cabbage.

NUTRITION (PER SERVE)

CALS	FAT	SAT FAT	PROTEIN	CARBS
274	8g	2g	27g	21g

○ FREEZABLE ○ GLUTEN FREE ● MAKE AHEAD ○ ONE POT ○ VEGAN ○ VEGO ○ YEAR-ROUND FAVE

★★★★★
This was delicious. I just made it in a pot on the stove. I used beef stock instead of water. Very easy, healthy meal. **HAMBLY**

15
mins prep

SLOW BEEF

PHO BO

Vietnamese pho is a traditional favourite in South-East Asia. When made in the slow cooker, the broth has loads of time to develop the flavour.

SERVES 6 **PREP** 20 mins (+ 1 hour soaking) **COOK** 10 hours 10 mins

1.2kg meaty beef bones or oxtail

1½ tbs sea salt

8 whole cloves

4 whole star anise

2 tsp whole coriander seeds

1 tsp fennel seeds

2 tsp cumin seeds

2 tsp peppercorns

2 brown onions, quartered

2 large carrots, cut into 5cm pieces

5 garlic cloves, peeled, bruised

8cm piece fresh ginger, peeled, cut into 2cm pieces

2 cinnamon sticks

2 tbs fish sauce, plus extra to taste

15g palm sugar, grated

2 tbs lime juice

250g pkt flat rice noodles

200-250g fillet steak, very thinly sliced

200g bean sprouts, trimmed

3 green shallots, thinly sliced

1-2 long fresh red chillies, thinly sliced

1½ cups mixed fresh herbs (coriander, Vietnamese mint, Thai basil)

Hoisin sauce and lime wedges, to serve

1 Place bones and 1 tbs sea salt in a large bowl. Cover with cold water. Set aside for 1 hour to soak. Drain. Rinse under cold running water. Transfer to the slow cooker.

2 Meanwhile, place the cloves, star anise, coriander, fennel, cumin and peppercorns in a piece of muslin. Tie to secure.

3 Add the onion, carrot, garlic, ginger, cinnamon, fish sauce, palm sugar, remaining salt and the spice pouch to the slow cooker. Add enough water to cover bones. Cover with the lid. Cook on Low for 8-10 hours or until meat is falling from the bone.

4 Use a slotted spoon to transfer solids to a bowl. Discard vegetables and spice pouch. Remove meat from bones and shred. Discard bones. Skim and discard fat from the surface of the stock. Stir in lime juice and shredded meat. Add extra fish sauce to taste. Keep warm.

5 Place the noodles in a heatproof bowl. Cover with boiling water. Soak for 5-10 minutes or until just tender. Drain. Divide noodles among serving bowls.

6 Place shredded meat on top of noodles. Ladle hot stock over. Top with bean sprouts, shallot, chilli and herbs. Serve with hoisin sauce and lime wedges.

NUTRITION (PER SERVE)

CALS	FAT	SAT FAT	PROTEIN	CARBS
413	11g	4g	31g	43g

○ FREEZABLE ○ GLUTEN FREE ● MAKE AHEAD ● ONE POT ○ VEGAN ○ VEGO ● YEAR-ROUND FAVE

LAMB SOUP WITH PUMPKIN

The Moroccan spices and rich vegies in this hearty soup add a flavoursome twist to the slow-cooked lamb.

SERVES 6 **PREP** 15 mins **COOK** 6 hours 30 mins

2 tsp Moroccan spice mix
6 French-trimmed lamb shanks
500g butternut pumpkin, peeled, deseeded, cut into 1cm pieces
500ml (2 cups) chicken stock
250g (1 cup) passata
400g can chickpeas, rinsed, drained
100g (½ cup) basmati rice
Fresh coriander leaves, to serve
Greek-style natural yoghurt, to serve

1 Place spice mix on a plate. Add the lamb shanks and toss to lightly coat.

2 Put the lamb, pumpkin, stock, 500ml (2 cups) water and passata into the slow cooker. Cover and cook on Low for 6 hours or until the lamb is falling off the bone. Use tongs to remove the bones and discard.

3 Add the chickpeas and rice. Cook for a further 30 minutes or until the rice is tender.

4 Ladle among serving bowls and top with the coriander. Serve with yoghurt.

COOK'S TIP

To reheat leftover soup, place in a saucepan and stir over medium-low heat until heated through. Add extra stock if necessary – the mixture thickens on standing.

NUTRITION (PER SERVE)

CALS	FAT	SAT FAT	PROTEIN	CARBS
410	6g	3g	41g	46g

★★★★★

Really yummy and a success with the whole family. I added onion and garlic and more than the recommended amount of spices (I made up my own Moroccan spice blend) and cooked it a bit longer than 6 hours to achieve 'falling off bone' lamb. Will make again. **KIMBOBOWEN**

● FREEZABLE ○ GLUTEN FREE ● MAKE AHEAD ● ONE POT ○ VEGAN ○ VEGO ○ YEAR-ROUND FAVE

BEAN SOUP WITH PANCETTA

This soup is perfect for chilly winter evenings – the borlotti beans add flavour and fibre and the toasts are a great accompaniment.

SERVES 4 **PREP** 15 mins (+ overnight soaking) **COOK** 7 hours 20 mins

190g (1 cup) dried borlotti beans
1 tsp extra virgin olive oil
1 large brown onion, finely chopped
4 celery sticks, finely chopped
1 large carrot, peeled, finely chopped
75g pancetta, finely chopped
3 garlic cloves, crushed
2 tsp finely chopped fresh rosemary
1 fresh long red chilli, deseeded, finely chopped
500ml (2 cups) salt-reduced chicken or vegetable stock (preferably homemade)
100g trimmed cavolo nero (Tuscan cabbage), chopped
4 slices rye bread, toasted
4 tbs fresh basil pesto
Baby herbs, to serve

1 Place beans in a bowl. Cover with cold water. Set aside for 8 hours or overnight to soak. Drain. Place in a saucepan. Cover with cold water. Bring to the boil over medium-high heat. Cook for 10 minutes. Drain well.

2 Heat the oil in a non-stick frying pan over medium heat. Cook the onion, celery, carrot and pancetta, stirring, for 5 minutes or until soft. Add the garlic, rosemary and chilli. Cook, stirring, for 1 minute or until aromatic.

3 Put the onion mixture, beans, stock and 500ml (2 cups) water in the slow cooker. Cover. Cook on Low for 6-7 hours. Stir the cavolo nero through and season with black pepper.

4 Spread toast with pesto. Divide soup among bowls. Top with herbs. Serve with toast.

COOK'S NOTE

Slow cookers are perfect for cooking dried legumes such as borlotti beans, because they take a long time to cook. They do need to be boiled first to destroy toxins.

NUTRITION (PER SERVE)

CALS	FAT	SAT FAT	PROTEIN	CARBS
366	9g	2g	20g	40g

○ FREEZABLE   ○ GLUTEN FREE   ● MAKE AHEAD   ○ ONE POT   ○ VEGAN   ○ VEGO   ○ YEAR-ROUND FAVE

STEWS

RICH IN FLAVOUR, THESE DISHES WILL FILL THE
KITCHEN WITH AMAZING AROMAS – AND ANTICIPATION.

POMEGRANATE LAMB SHANKS

Full of aromatic herbs and spices, this great version of slow-cooked lamb shanks is set to become your go-to winter warmer.

SERVES 6   **PREP** 30 mins   **COOK** 6 hours 10 mins

2 tbs extra virgin olive oil

6 lamb shanks

1 large brown onion, thinly sliced

4 garlic cloves, crushed

2 tsp ground coriander

1 tsp ground cinnamon

1 tsp ground allspice

1 tbs finely chopped
fresh rosemary

⅔ cup whole cranberry sauce

250ml (1 cup) pomegranate juice

250ml (1 cup) gluten-free
chicken stock

2 tbs pomegranate molasses

40g (¼ cup) dried cranberries

500g brussels sprouts, halved

50g butter, chopped

750ml (3 cups) milk

260g (1½ cups) instant polenta

2 tbs chopped continental
parsley leaves

2 tbs natural flaked almonds, toasted

1 tbs pistachio kernels,
coarsely chopped

1 Heat half the oil in a large non-stick frying pan over high heat. Cook shanks, in batches, for 5-7 minutes or until browned all over. Transfer to the slow cooker.

2 Heat remaining oil in the pan over medium-high heat. Add onion. Cook, stirring, for 5 minutes or until softened. Add garlic, coriander, cinnamon, allspice and rosemary. Cook, stirring, for 1 minute or until fragrant.

3 Add sauce, juice, stock and molasses. Bring to the boil, then carefully pour over the lamb shank in the slow cooker. Cover and cook on Low for 6 hours, adding the cranberries for the final 2 hours of cooking.

4 Meanwhile, cook the sprouts in a saucepan of boiling water for 2 minutes or until almost tender. Drain well. Heat half the butter in a large frying pan over medium-high heat. Add sprouts. Cook, stirring occasionally, for 8-10 minutes or until golden and crisp. Season.

5 Combine milk and 500ml (2 cups) water in a medium saucepan. Bring to the boil over medium-high heat. Slowly pour in polenta, stirring constantly. Reduce heat to medium-low. Cook, stirring, for 5 minutes or until thickened. Add remaining butter. Stir until melted. Season.

6 Combine parsley, pistachios and almonds in a small bowl. Divide polenta among serving bowls and place a lamb shank and sprouts on top. Drizzle with pan juices and scatter with the parsley mixture.

NUTRITION (PER SERVE)

CALS	FAT	SAT FAT	PROTEIN	CARBS
741	30g	12g	42g	72g

○ FREEZABLE   ● GLUTEN FREE   ● MAKE AHEAD   ○ ONE POT   ○ VEGAN   ○ VEGO   ○ YEAR-ROUND FAVE

30
mins prep

BEEF BRISKET
BOURGUIGNON

Use budget-friendly brisket to create this classic French country-style dish and let the rich flavours develop in the slow cooker.

SERVES 6 **PREP** 20 mins **COOK** 6 hours 20 mins

2 tsp extra virgin olive oil
1.5kg beef brisket
12 French shallots, peeled
200g streaky bacon, halved lengthways, chopped
3 garlic cloves, crushed
6 sprigs fresh thyme, plus extra to serve
1 dried bay leaf
250ml (1 cup) red wine
125ml (½ cup) beef stock
1 tbs tomato paste
2 carrots, thickly sliced
200g swiss brown mushrooms, halved
200g button mushrooms
Steamed green beans and mashed potato, to serve

1 Heat half the oil in a frying pan over medium-high heat. Cook beef for 5 minutes each side or until browned. Transfer to the slow cooker.

2 Reduce heat to medium. Add remaining oil to the pan. Add shallots and bacon. Cook, stirring, for 5 minutes or until shallots soften. Add garlic and thyme. Cook for 1 minute. Transfer to the slow cooker. Add the bay leaf, wine, stock and tomato paste. Top with the carrot and mushroom. Cover and cook on Low for 6 hours or until the beef is very tender.

3 Remove and discard bay leaf. Using 2 forks, shred meat. Season. Serve with green beans, mashed potato and extra thyme sprigs.

NUTRITION (PER SERVE)

CALS	FAT	SAT FAT	PROTEIN	CARBS
758	42g	16g	63g	20g

COOK'S NOTE

If you prefer, leave out the red wine and use an extra 250ml (1 cup) stock instead.

Secret Hack

Make it gluten-free! Check the ingredients of the stock, tomato paste and the bacon if you want to serve a gluten-free meal.

● FREEZABLE ○ GLUTEN FREE ● MAKE AHEAD ○ ONE POT ○ VEGAN ○ VEGO ○ YEAR-ROUND FAVE

20
mins prep

89

ITALIAN BEEF WITH GNOCCHI

Rich, warm and comforting, this modern and practical twist on an Italian favourite is sure to become part of your regular repertoire.

SERVES 6 **PREP** 15 mins **COOK** 8 hours 15 mins

2 tbs olive oil

1.25kg chuck steak, trimmed, cut into 3cm chunks

1 brown onion, chopped

2 carrots, chopped

2 celery sticks, sliced

2 garlic cloves, crushed

15g chopped dried porcini mushrooms

375ml (1½ cups) beef stock

400g can diced tomatoes

1 fresh or dried bay leaf

500g pkt potato gnocchi

Chopped fresh continental parsley, to serve

1 Heat 1 tbs oil in a large non-stick frying pan over medium-high heat. Cook the steak in 2-3 batches, turning occasionally, for 3 minutes or until browned. Transfer to a plate.

2 Reduce the heat to medium. Heat the remaining oil in the pan and cook the onion, carrot and celery, stirring occasionally, for 5 minutes or until soft and light golden. Stir in the garlic and cook for 1 minute. Transfer meat and vegetables to the slow cooker.

3 Stir in the mushrooms, stock, tomatoes and bay leaf. Cover and cook on Low for 7 hours.

4 Briefly uncover slow cooker and stir in gnocchi. Cover again and cook for 1 hour. Sprinkle with chopped parsley.

COOK'S NOTE

Serve with crunchy slices of ciabatta to mop up the sauce.

NUTRITION (PER SERVE)

CALS	FAT	SAT FAT	PROTEIN	CARBS
497	20g	7g	42g	36g

○ FREEZABLE ○ GLUTEN FREE ● **MAKE AHEAD** ○ ONE POT ○ VEGAN ○ VEGO ○ YEAR-ROUND FAVE

CLASSIC APRICOT
CHICKEN

This ever-popular family favourite uses chicken thigh cutlets,
so it's budget-friendly and super simple to pull together.

SERVES 4 **PREP** 15 mins **COOK** 6 hours 10 mins

8 small chicken thigh cutlets, excess
   fat trimmed
40g pkt French onion soup mix
410g can apricot halves, drained
405ml can apricot nectar
1 tbs cornflour
Steamed rice, steamed broccolini,
   fresh thyme sprigs (optional),
   to serve

1 Heat a large non-stick frying pan over medium-high heat. Add half the chicken, skin-side down, and cook for 3 minutes or until golden. Turn and cook for a further 3 minutes. Transfer to the slow cooker. Repeat with the remaining chicken.

2 Sprinkle the soup mix over the chicken. Add the apricot halves and pour the apricot nectar over. Cover and cook on Low for 6 hours.

3 Use tongs to transfer the chicken to a warm oven tray and cover with foil to keep warm (alternatively, pop the tray into a preheated 180°C/160°C fan forced oven, without the foil, for 5-10 minutes). Increase the slow cooker heat to High. Stir the cornflour with 1 tbs of water until smooth. Add to the slow cooker and stir to combine. Cover and heat for 5 minutes. Stir again.

4 Serve the chicken and apricots with rice and broccolini, and scattered with thyme, if using.

COOK'S NOTE

To reduce the fat content of this dish you could remove the skin from the chicken. Add 1 tbs extra virgin olive oil to brown.

NUTRITION (PER SERVE)

CALS	FAT	SAT FAT	PROTEIN	CARBS
1005	38g	12g	64g	98g

● FREEZABLE ○ GLUTEN FREE ● MAKE AHEAD ○ ONE POT ○ VEGAN ○ VEGO ● YEAR-ROUND FAVE

15
mins prep

93

PULLED VEGIES IN TORTILLAS

This vegan version of pulled pork is full of smoky spices and will keep even meatlovers happy (and full).

SERVES 6 **PREP** 5 mins **COOK** 6 hours 35 mins

60ml (¼ cup) peanut oil
2 (about 600g) eggplant, halved
    lengthways
400g can chopped tomatoes
125ml (½ cup) smoky barbecue
    sauce, plus extra, to serve
    (optional)
1 tbs brown sugar
250g pkt rainbow coleslaw mixture
400g can black beans, rinsed, drained
Tortillas, grilled, to serve
90g (⅓ cup) vegan mayonnaise
Fresh coriander sprigs, to serve

1 Heat the oil in a large non-stick frying pan over high heat. Add the eggplant, cut-side down and cook for 5 minutes or until golden. Place, cut-side up, in a slow cooker.

2 Add the tomato, barbecue sauce and brown sugar to the slow cooker. Season. Cover and cook on Low for 6 hours. Use tongs and a fork to shred the eggplant. Add the coleslaw and the beans and stir to coat. Cook on Low for a further 30 minutes.

3 Serve the pulled vegetables in warmed tortillas. Drizzle with mayo, extra barbecue sauce, if using, and scatter coriander sprigs over.

COOK'S NOTE

Replace the black beans with red kidney beans, if you like. You could also add a 300g can corn kernels, drained.

NUTRITION (PER SERVE)

CALS	FAT	SAT FAT	PROTEIN	CARBS
456	23g	4g	10g	49g

Secret Hack

Budget saver! Make your own coleslaw with a mixture of shredded purple and green cabbage combined with grated carrot.

○ FREEZABLE   ○ GLUTEN FREE   ● MAKE AHEAD   ○ ONE POT   ● VEGAN   ● VEGO   ● YEAR-ROUND FAVE

APRICOT CHICKEN
TAGINE

Moroccan flavours combine to create a rich and satisfying dish with only 15 minutes of prep time.

SERVES 4 **PREP** 15 mins **COOK** 6 hour 50 mins

2 tbs extra virgin olive oil
8 small skinless chicken thigh cutlets
35g (¼ cup) plain flour
1 large brown onion, halved, thickly sliced
2 garlic cloves, crushed
1 tsp ground cumin
1 tsp ground coriander
1 tsp ground turmeric
1 cinnamon stick
375ml (1½ cups) chicken stock
410g can apricot halves
400g can chickpeas, rinsed, drained
150g green beans, trimmed, halved
½ cup fresh coriander leaves
1 fresh long red chilli, thinly sliced
35g (¼ cup) pistachio kernels, toasted, coarsely chopped
Couscous, to serve

1 Heat half the oil in a large frying pan over medium-high heat. Toss chicken in flour to coat, shaking off excess. Cook chicken, in batches, turning, for 5 minutes or until browned all over. Transfer to the slow cooker.

2 Heat remaining oil in same pan. Cook onion, stirring, for 5 minutes or until softened. Add garlic, cumin, ground coriander and turmeric. Cook, stirring, for 1 minute or until fragrant. Add cinnamon stick and stock. Season with pepper. Bring to the boil.

3 Drain apricots, reserving 125ml (½ cup) juice. Add the chickpeas and reserved apricot juice to the slow cooker. Refrigerate apricot halves until required. Pour onion mixture over chicken mixture in slow cooker. Cover with the lid and cook on Low for 6 hours (or High for 3 hours). Add beans and reserved apricot halves. Cook on High for a further 30 minutes.

4 Scatter coriander leaves, chilli and pistachio over tagine. Serve with couscous.

COOK'S NOTE

Discard the cinnamon stick before serving.

NUTRITION (PER SERVE)

CALS	FAT	SAT FAT	PROTEIN	CARBS
630	21g	4g	38g	67g

● FREEZABLE ○ GLUTEN FREE ● MAKE AHEAD ○ ONE POT ○ VEGAN ○ VEGO ● YEAR-ROUND FAVE

SLOW-COOKER BEEF TERIYAKI

With a Japanese-style marinade made from soy sauce, mirin, beef stock and sake, this dish will melt in your mouth.

SERVES 8 **PREP** 10 mins **COOK** 8 hours 15 mins

1 tbs extra virgin olive oil
1.5kg piece blade or topside beef
250ml (1 cup) beef stock
80ml (⅓ cup) light soy sauce
60ml (¼ cup) mirin seasoning
60ml (¼ cup) cooking sake
2 tbs brown sugar
2 garlic cloves, crushed
2 tsp finely grated ginger
Toasted sesame seeds, to serve
Steamed rice, to serve
Sliced green shallots and red chilli
  (optional), to serve

1 Heat oil in a large non-stick frying pan over medium-high heat. Add the beef and cook, turning often, for 10 minutes or until browned. Transfer to the slow cooker.

2 Place the stock, soy sauce, mirin, sake, sugar, garlic and ginger in a jug. Stir to dissolve the sugar. Pour over the beef. Cover and cook on Low, turning the meat occasionally, for 8 hours or until very tender

3 Transfer the beef to a large plate. Use 2 forks to coarsely shred. Return the beef to the slow cooker to cover in sauce. Divide beef among serving plates. Sprinkle with sesame seeds. Serve with steamed rice, scattered with sliced shallots and chilli, if using.

COOK'S NOTE

Steam some Asian greens such as bok choy or choy sum as a quick side dish.

NUTRITION (PER SERVE)

CALS	FAT	SAT FAT	PROTEIN	CARBS
349	15g	5g	41g	12g

★★★★★ *Quick to prepare, set and forget until dinner... I used large chuck steak cuts instead and after 8 hours it fell apart, reduced the juices and made a delicious sauce. Will be having again.* **JULES0217**

● FREEZABLE ○ GLUTEN FREE ● MAKE AHEAD ○ ONE POT ○ VEGAN ○ VEGO ● YEAR-ROUND FAVE

RUSTIC ITALIAN CHICKEN CASSEROLE

This winter fave is made easy in the slow cooker. Full of rich Mediterranean flavours on a tomato base, it's sure to join the weekly repertoire.

SERVES 6 **PREP** 15 mins **COOK** 8 hours 25 mins

2 tbs extra virgin olive oil
1 brown onion, chopped
12 skinless chicken thigh cutlets
2 celery sticks, chopped
2 carrots, chopped
3 garlic cloves, finely chopped
700g btl passata
125ml (½ cup) salt-reduced
   chicken stock
1 tsp dried oregano
2 tsp caster sugar
500g mushrooms, sliced
40g (¼ cup) pitted kalamata olives
200g green beans, steamed
Crusty bread, to serve

1 Heat half the oil in a large frying pan over medium heat. Add the onion. Cook, stirring, for 5 minutes or until softened. Transfer to the slow cooker.

2 Heat remaining oil in the pan over medium-high heat. Cook the chicken, in batches, for 2 minutes each side or until just browned all over. Add to the slow cooker.

3 Add celery, carrot, garlic, passata, stock, oregano and sugar to slow cooker. Stir to combine. Cover. Cook on High for 4 hours (or Low for 8 hours), adding the mushroom in the last 30 minutes of cooking. Season.

4 Add olives to the chicken mixture and stir to combine. Serve casserole with beans and crusty bread.

COOK'S NOTE

If you have leftovers, cool, then place into an airtight container. Refrigerate for up to 3 days or freeze for up to 3 months.

NUTRITION (PER SERVE)

CALS	FAT	SAT FAT	PROTEIN	CARBS
375	17g	4g	37g	13g

★★★★★

Super easy and great for midweek meals. Fussy hubby loved it and one of the few ways I can get him to eat extra vegies. **JESTER123**

● FREEZABLE   ○ GLUTEN FREE   ● MAKE AHEAD   ○ ONE POT   ○ VEGAN   ○ VEGO   ○ YEAR-ROUND FAVE

PULLED TURKEY WITH PINEAPPLE

The rich taste of turkey drumsticks balances the unexpected sweetness of pineapple for a blend of flavours.

SERVES 4 **PREP** 15 mins **COOK** 6 hours 15 mins

2 tsp olive oil
2 (1.5kg) turkey drumsticks
1 brown onion, halved, thinly sliced
2 red capsicums, thinly sliced
2 garlic cloves, thinly sliced
3cm piece fresh ginger, peeled,
    finely chopped
440g can pineapple pieces in juice
400g can diced tomatoes
1 tbs tomato sauce
1 tbs Worcestershire sauce
Steamed rice, sugar snap peas and
    fresh coriander sprigs, to serve

1 Heat half the oil in a large deep non-stick frying pan over medium-high heat. Add turkey. Cook, turning occasionally, for 6 to 8 minutes or until browned all over. Transfer to the slow cooker.

2 Reduce heat to medium. Heat remaining oil in pan. Add onion and capsicum. Cook, stirring often, for 5 minutes or until softened. Add garlic and ginger. Cook for 1 minute or until fragrant. Add pineapple pieces and juice, tomato, tomato sauce and Worcestershire sauce. Stir to combine. Season. Pour tomato mixture over turkey.

3 Cover with the lid. Cook on Low for 6 hours or until the turkey is tender, turning halfway through cooking time.

4 Remove turkey from sauce. Discard skin and bones. Shred meat. Return to sauce. Serve with steamed rice, sugar snap peas and coriander sprigs.

COOK'S NOTE

Turkey is a healthy meat, high in protein and low in fat, and full of valuable nutrients. It's also delicious!

NUTRITION (PER SERVE)

CALS	FAT	SAT FAT	PROTEIN	CARBS
821	21g	6g	76g	76g

○ FREEZABLE ○ GLUTEN FREE ● MAKE AHEAD ○ ONE POT ○ VEGAN ○ VEGO ● YEAR-ROUND FAVE

CUBAN PULLED BEEF

Served with a zesty chimichurri as a dressing, this melt-in-your-mouth dish evokes beachside holidays and Latin American flavours.

SERVES 8   **PREP** 20 mins   **COOK** 8 hours 15 mins

1 tbs extra virgin olive oil
1.5kg gravy beef
1 brown onion, finely chopped
2 red capsicums, finely chopped
2 garlic cloves, crushed
2 tsp dried oregano
2 dried bay leaves
2 tsp caster sugar
1 tsp dried chilli flakes
1 tsp ground allspice
700g jar gluten-free passata
80ml (⅓ cup) red wine vinegar
400g (2 cups) white long-grain rice
400g can black beans, drained, rinsed
2 tbs chopped fresh coriander
1 green shallot, finely chopped
2 tbs fresh lime juice
Lime wedges, to serve

CHIMICHURRI
1½ cups fresh continental
   parsley leaves
½ cup fresh coriander leaves
½ cup fresh oregano leaves
2 garlic cloves, halved
60ml (¼ cup) extra virgin olive oil
2 tbs red wine vinegar

1 Heat oil in a frying pan over medium-high heat. Cook beef for 5 minutes or until browned. Transfer to the slow cooker. Top with onion, capsicum, garlic, oregano, bay leaves, sugar, chilli, allspice, passata and vinegar. Season. Cover and cook on Low for 8 hours, turning beef in sauce halfway through cooking.

2 To make chimichurri, process the herbs and garlic in a small food processor until finely chopped. Add the oil and vinegar. Process until combined. Set aside.

3 Cook the rice following packet directions, adding the beans in the last 2 minutes of cooking. Drain. Transfer to a bowl. Stir in coriander and green shallot. Season. Using 2 forks, shred beef. Stir in lime juice. Serve beef with rice, chimichurri and lime wedges.

COOK'S NOTE

If you can't find black beans, you can use red kidney beans instead.

NUTRITION (PER SERVE)

CALS	FAT	SAT FAT	PROTEIN	CARBS
705	28g	8g	48g	59g

● FREEZABLE ● GLUTEN FREE ● MAKE AHEAD ○ ONE POT ○ VEGAN ○ VEGO ● YEAR-ROUND FAVE

CHICKEN AND MUSHROOM
STROGANOFF

Made with chicken instead of the traditional beef, the flavours of mushroom and paprika make this a rich and satisfying slow-cooked stew.

SERVES 4 **PREP** 15 mins **COOK** 6 hours 15 mins

2 tbs olive oil
8 small chicken thigh cutlets (1.2kg), skin removed, fat trimmed
1 brown onion, halved, thinly sliced
2 garlic cloves, crushed
2 tbs tomato paste
2 tbs plain flour
2 tsp paprika
500ml (2 cups) chicken stock
300g button mushrooms, halved
Chopped fresh chives, to serve
Sour cream, to serve (optional)

1 Heat 1 tbs oil in a large non-stick frying pan over medium heat. Cook the chicken, flesh side down, for 4 minutes or until well browned. Turn and cook for 2 minutes. Transfer to a plate.

2 Heat the remaining oil in the pan. Cook the onion for 5 minutes or until light golden and softened slightly. Stir in garlic, then tomato paste, flour and paprika. Cook, stirring, for 1 minute. Add the stock a little at a time, stirring to combine evenly between each addition. Bring to the boil then pour into the slow cooker.

3 Place the chicken in the slow cooker, flesh-side up. Cover and cook on Low for 6 hours, adding the mushrooms in the last hour of cooking, or until the chicken is very tender. Sprinkle with chives. Serve with sour cream, if using.

COOK'S NOTE

Serve with mashed potato and green beans, if you like.

NUTRITION (PER SERVE)

CALS	FAT	SAT FAT	PROTEIN	CARBS
497	20g	7g	42g	36g

● FREEZABLE ○ GLUTEN FREE ● MAKE AHEAD ○ ONE POT ○ VEGAN ○ VEGO ○ YEAR-ROUND FAVE

15
mins prep

LAMB SHANKS WITH GUINNESS

Adding Guinness to these shanks gives the sauce a rich stout flavour.
Serve with creamy mashed potato for the full experience.

SERVES 4 **PREP** 20 mins **COOK** 6 hours 15 mins

1 tsp olive oil
4 French-trimmed lamb shanks
1 leek, trimmed, thinly sliced
2 carrots, diced
2 garlic cloves, thinly sliced
2 tbs tomato paste
500ml (2 cups) beef stock
250ml (1 cup) Guinness
Mashed potato or crusty bread and
    steamed green beans, to serve

1 Heat oil in a large, deep non-stick frying pan over medium-high heat. Season lamb. Add to pan. Cook, turning often, for 6-8 minutes or until browned all over. Transfer to the bowl of a slow cooker.

2 Reduce heat to medium. Add leek and carrot. Cook, stirring often, for 5 minutes or until softened. Add garlic. Cook for 1 minute or until fragrant. Add tomato paste. Cook, stirring constantly, for 30 seconds. Add stock and Guinness. Season. Pour over lamb. Cover with lid. Cook on Low for 6 hours or until lamb is tender.

3 Serve lamb shanks and sauce with mashed potato or bread and beans.

NUTRITION (PER SERVE)

CALS	FAT	SAT FAT	PROTEIN	CARBS
522	14g	6g	58g	31g

COOK'S NOTE

To reduce the fat, transfer mixture from the slow cooker to a large heatproof bowl. Refrigerate overnight or until fat sets on the top. Remove and discard fat. Reheat mixture in a saucepan over medium heat. Cook for 15 minutes or until heated through.

● FREEZABLE　○ GLUTEN FREE　● MAKE AHEAD　○ ONE POT　○ VEGAN　○ VEGO　○ YEAR-ROUND FAVE

STEWS

20 mins prep

★★★★★
Makes a great easy meal as you can put it all in and forget.
Even better flavours the next day. SONYAMAREE

SPICY CHICKEN MEATBALLS

These kid-friendly chicken meatballs are guaranteed to hit the spot to create a simple midweek meal.

SERVES 6 **PREP** 20 mins (+ 10 mins soaking) **COOK** 4 hours 25 mins

1 slice wholemeal bread, crusts
   removed, torn
2 tbs milk
500g chicken mince
1 egg white
35g (⅓ cup) dried breadcrumbs
1 tsp ground coriander
1 tsp sweet paprika
1 tsp ground cumin
1 tsp ground ginger
1 brown onion, finely chopped
3 garlic cloves, crushed
2 tbs extra virgin olive oil
2 tbs tomato paste
700g btl passata
2 tbs honey
2 zucchini, halved, thickly sliced
80g (⅔ cup) frozen peas
Couscous, plain Greek-style yoghurt
   and fresh coriander sprigs, to serve

1 Place bread and milk in a large bowl. Set aside for 10 minutes to soak. Add mince, egg white, breadcrumbs, ground coriander, sweet paprika, cumin, ground ginger, half the onion and half the garlic to the bread mixture. Season. Mix well to combine. Roll level tablespoons of mixture into balls.

2 Heat oil in a large frying pan over medium heat. Cook meatballs in 2 batches, turning, for 2-3 minutes or until just browned. Transfer to the slow cooker.

3 Add remaining onion and garlic to pan. Cook, stirring, for 5 minutes or until onion softens. Stir in tomato paste, passata, honey and 125ml (½ cup) water. Transfer mixture to the slow cooker. Add zucchini. Cover and cook on Low for 4 hours or until meatballs are tender and cooked through.

4 Stir in the peas. Cook for a further 10 minutes. Season. Serve with couscous, yoghurt and fresh coriander.

COOK'S NOTE

Add extra zing for grown-up palates by replacing the sweet paprika with hot paprika and adding dried chilli flakes to the tomato sauce mixture.

NUTRITION (PER SERVE)

CALS	FAT	SAT FAT	PROTEIN	CARBS
523	15g	4g	30g	64g

★★★★★ *Kids loved it and it's easy to make.* **AMANDAMATHER**

● FREEZABLE ○ GLUTEN FREE ● MAKE AHEAD ○ ONE POT ○ VEGAN ○ VEGO ● YEAR-ROUND FAVE

CLASSIC VIETNAMESE

BO KHO

This Vietnamese classic of braised beef (bò kho) is served with succulent rice noodles – simple comfort food without being too heavy.

SERVES 6   **PREP** 15 mins   **COOK** 4 hours

1.2kg beef brisket
2 carrots, quartered lengthways, cut into 3cm lengths
2 garlic cloves, crushed
3 lemongrass stems, pale section only, finely chopped
90g (⅓ cup) tomato paste
2 tbs fish sauce
1 tsp Chinese five-spice powder
750ml (3 cups) salt-reduced beef stock
200g packet dried rice noodles
195g (3 cups) bean sprouts, trimmed
½ small red onion, thinly sliced
Fresh mint leaves, fresh coriander leaves, chilli oil and lime wedges, to serve

1 Trim beef of all fat and sinew. Cut into 3cm pieces. Place beef, carrot, garlic, lemongrass, tomato paste, fish sauce, five spice and stock in slow cooker. Cover and cook on Low for 4 hours (or on High for 2 hours).

2 Cook noodles following packet directions. Drain. Divide noodles among serving bowls. Top with beef mixture. Sprinkle with bean sprouts, onion, mint and coriander. Drizzle with chilli oil. Serve with lime wedges.

NUTRITION (PER SERVE)

CALS	FAT	SAT FAT	PROTEIN	CARBS
486	18g	6g	43g	33g

COOK'S NOTE

Replace red onion with thinly sliced green shallots if you prefer a less pungent onion flavour.

Secret Hack

Make it gluten-free! Check the ingredients of the tomato paste and stock if you want to serve a gluten-free meal.

○ FREEZABLE   ○ GLUTEN FREE   ● MAKE AHEAD   ○ ONE POT   ○ VEGAN   ○ VEGO   ● YEAR-ROUND FAVE

15
mins prep

113

MIDDLE EASTERN CHICKPEA STEW

High in fibre and low in fat and calories, this hearty stew
is full of flavour and aromatic spices – and only three steps!

SERVES 4 **PREP** 10 mins **COOK** 6 hours

100g (½ cup) dried chickpeas,
  rinsed, drained
400g orange sweet potato,
  peeled, cut into 3cm pieces
1 brown onion, finely chopped
1 large carrot, thickly sliced
110g (½ cup) dried apricots
8 fresh dates, pitted
500ml (2 cups) vegetable stock
400g can chopped tomatoes
3 tsp Moroccan
  seasoning paste
2 zucchini, halved lengthways,
  thickly sliced
Cooked Israeli (pearl) couscous and
  fresh coriander leaves, to serve
Plain yoghurt, to serve (optional)

1 Place chickpeas, sweet potato, onion, carrot, apricots,
dates, stock, tomatoes and seasoning in the slow cooker.
Stir to combine.

2 Cover with the lid. Cook on Low for 6 hours (or on
High for 3 hours), adding the zucchini halfway through
cooking. Season.

3 Divide stew among bowls with couscous and scatter
with coriander leaves. Serve with yoghurt, if using.

NUTRITION (PER SERVE)

CALS	FAT	SAT FAT	PROTEIN	CARBS
308	3g	0.5g	11g	54g

COOK'S NOTE

Israeli couscous
is larger than
regular couscous
and needs to
be cooked in
boiling water for
8-10 minutes
until tender.

★★★★★

*Had serious doubts – I couldn't find Moroccan paste and had
to substitute Moroccan seasoning, but it turned out awesome!
I added garlic, ground cumin and onion powder to make up for
lack of paste and the flavour was amazing.* **JESSICA WILSON**

● FREEZABLE ○ GLUTEN FREE ● MAKE AHEAD ● ONE POT ○ VEGAN ● VEGO ● YEAR-ROUND FAVE

MOROCCAN BEEF AND BARLEY

Warm and comforting, this hearty beef stew has harissa for heat and spice, combined with raisins for fruity flavour.

SERVES 4 **PREP** 20 mins **COOK** 6 hours 12 mins

3 tsp extra virgin olive oil
600g beef chuck steak, trimmed, cut into 3cm pieces
1 brown onion, chopped
3 carrots, halved lengthways, sliced
2 garlic cloves, thinly sliced
1 tbs Middle Eastern spice blend (harissa)
400g can diced tomatoes
95g (½ cup) raisins
75g (⅓ cup) pearl barley
Steamed rice, plain Greek-style yoghurt and fresh coriander sprigs, to serve

1 Heat 1 tsp oil in a large deep non-stick frying pan over medium-high heat. Season beef. Add half the beef to the pan. Cook for 3 minutes or until browned all over. Transfer to the slow cooker. Repeat with half the remaining oil and remaining beef.

2 Reduce heat to medium. Heat remaining oil in pan. Add onion and carrot. Cook, stirring often, for 5 minutes or until softened. Add garlic and spice blend. Cook, stirring, for 1 minute or until fragrant. Add tomatoes and 375ml (1½ cups) cold water. Season. Pour over beef. Cover and cook on Low for 4 hours. Add raisins, barley and 250ml (1 cup) cold water. Cover. Cook for a further 2 hours until beef is tender.

3 Spoon beef over rice. Serve topped with yoghurt and scattered with coriander.

COOK'S NOTE

The dried spice blend we used has a milder flavour than harissa paste, which is much spicier.

NUTRITION (PER SERVE)

CALS	FAT	SAT FAT	PROTEIN	CARBS
712	17g	6g	42g	90g

○ FREEZABLE ○ GLUTEN FREE ● MAKE AHEAD ○ ONE POT ○ VEGAN ○ VEGO ○ YEAR-ROUND FAVE

SLOW-COOKER BEEF GOULASH

Paprika – and time – is the key to a successful goulash and this one, served with sour cream and fettuccine, wins on both counts.

SERVES 4 (with leftovers) **PREP** 15 mins **COOK** 8 hours 10 mins

2 tbs extra virgin olive oil
1 brown onion, chopped
1.5kg beef chuck steak, trimmed, cut into 3cm pieces
2 tbs tomato paste
2½ tbs sweet paprika
80ml (⅓ cup) salt-reduced beef stock
2 red capsicums, cut into 2cm pieces
400g can diced tomatoes
500g cup mushrooms, sliced
1½ tbs cornflour
85g (⅓ cup) light sour cream
Fettuccine and chopped fresh continental parsley, to serve

1 Heat half the oil in a large frying pan over medium heat. Add onion. Cook, stirring, for 5 minutes or until softened. Transfer to the slow cooker.

2 Heat remaining oil in pan over medium-high heat. Cook beef, in batches, for 3-4 minutes or until browned.

3 Return beef to pan. Add tomato paste and paprika. Cook for 1 minute or until beef is coated. Add stock. Bring to a simmer. Transfer to the slow cooker. Add capsicum and tomatoes. Season. Stir to combine. Cover and cook on Low for 8 hours (or High for 4 hours), adding mushroom in the last 30 minutes of cooking time.

4 Serve goulash with sour cream, fettuccine and chopped fresh parsley.

COOK'S NOTE

Spoon leftovers into an airtight container. Refrigerate for up to 3 days or freeze for up to 3 months.

NUTRITION (PER SERVE)

CALS	FAT	SAT FAT	PROTEIN	CARBS
913	30g	10g	74g	80g

● FREEZABLE ○ GLUTEN FREE ● MAKE AHEAD ○ ONE POT ○ VEGAN ○ VEGO ○ YEAR-ROUND FAVE

15
mins prep

SLOW-COOKED COQ AU VIN

This classic French casserole is the perfect weekend entertainer with aromatic herbs and a red wine-infused marinade.

SERVES 4 **PREP** 25 mins (+ cooling & 3 hours marinating) **COOK** 8 hours 55 mins

1.6kg whole chicken, quartered and wingtips removed, or 4 marylands
200g speck, cut into small strips
2 garlic cloves, crushed
60ml (¼ cup) brandy
40g (¼ cup) plain flour
500ml (2 cups) chicken stock
100g butter, chopped
8 French shallots, peeled
1 tbs caster sugar
2 tbs olive oil
300g button mushrooms, trimmed
2 tbs chopped fresh continental parsley, fresh thyme sprigs, to serve

MARINADE
750ml (3 cups) pinot noir
2 carrots, peeled, thickly sliced
2 celery sticks, trimmed, thickly sliced
1 brown onion, cut into wedges
3 garlic cloves, crushed
3 French shallots, peeled, halved
2 tsp black peppercorns
2 dried bay leaves
10 sprigs fresh thyme
1 tsp salt

1 For the marinade, place all the ingredients in a large saucepan over medium-high heat. Bring to the boil. Set aside to cool.

2 Place chicken and marinade in a bowl. Cover with plastic wrap and refrigerate for 3 hours to allow flavours to develop. Remove chicken from marinade and pat dry with paper towel. Strain marinade into a bowl. Reserve vegetable mixture.

3 Heat a large frying pan over medium heat. Add the speck and cook, stirring occasionally, for 3 minutes or until the fat melts and speck is golden. Transfer speck to a plate lined with paper towel and set aside until needed.

4 Return pan to medium-high heat and cook chicken in 2 batches, for 3 minutes each side until browned. Transfer to the slow cooker. Drain all but 2 tbs fat from the pan, then return to heat. Add the garlic and reserved vegetable mixture and cook, stirring occasionally, for 6 minutes or until soft. Add the brandy and use a long match to carefully ignite. Allow the flame to burn out, then stir in flour. Gradually stir in stock, then reserved marinade. Transfer to the slow cooker with the chicken. Cover and cook on Low for 6-8 hours or until chicken is very tender.

5 Meanwhile, melt 50g butter in a large saucepan over medium-high heat. Add the shallots and sugar and cook, stirring occasionally, for 5 minutes or until the shallots are caramelised. Add 125ml (½ cup) water and bring to the boil. Simmer for 8 minutes or until the liquid reduces.

6 Heat oil and remaining butter in a frying pan over high heat. Cook mushrooms, tossing, for 5 minutes or until golden. Season.

7 Add speck, shallot mixture and mushrooms to the slow cooker. Cover and cook for a further 30 minutes. Season. Scatter with parsley and thyme.

NUTRITION (PER SERVE)

CALS	FAT	SAT FAT	PROTEIN	CARBS
1221	80g	32g	63g	20g

● FREEZABLE ○ GLUTEN FREE ● MAKE AHEAD ○ ONE POT ○ VEGAN ○ VEGO ○ YEAR-ROUND FAVE

★★★★★ *This is absolutely delicious.* **ROBYNS1**

CARAMEL PORK WITH ASIAN GREENS

Asian flavours such as ginger, lime and sweet chilli, give this succulent pork a zesty lift.

SERVES 6 **PREP** 20 mins **COOK** 6 hours 15 mins

1.8kg boneless pork shoulder
2 tbs plain flour
2 tbs vegetable oil
2 Asian shallots, thinly sliced
3cm piece ginger, cut into
  thin matchsticks
2 garlic cloves, thinly sliced
2 tbs sweet chilli sauce
185ml (¾ cup) salt-reduced
  chicken stock
2 tbs lime juice
1 tbs fish sauce
60ml (¼ cup) kecap manis
2 kaffir lime leaves, finely shredded
Steamed rice and Asian greens,
  to serve

1 Remove netting or string from pork. Cut rind and any excess fat from pork and discard. Cut pork into 8 large pieces. Place in a large sealable plastic bag with flour. Season with pepper. Seal. Shake to coat.

2 Heat half the oil in a large frying pan. Cook pork, in batches, for 5 minutes or until browned all over. Transfer to the slow cooker.

3 Heat remaining oil in pan. Add shallot, ginger and garlic. Cook, stirring, for 3 minutes or until softened. Transfer to the slow cooker. Add sweet chilli sauce, stock, lime juice, fish sauce, kecap manis and lime leaves. Stir to combine. Cover with lid. Cook on Low for 6 hours or until pork is very tender.

4 Remove pork from sauce. Coarsely shred into large pieces. Serve pork on steamed rice with Asian greens. Drizzle with sauce.

COOK'S NOTE

Browning meat before it goes into the slow cooker adds an extra depth of flavour.

NUTRITION (PER SERVE)

CALS	FAT	SAT FAT	PROTEIN	CARBS
549	23g	7g	46g	40g

○ FREEZABLE ○ GLUTEN FREE ● MAKE AHEAD ○ ONE POT ○ VEGAN ○ VEGO ● YEAR-ROUND FAVE

20
mins prep

Secret Hack
Budget saver! Replace the pork shoulder
with 2kg of chicken drumsticks.

FRENCH BURGUNDY BEEF

Use the stove top (and a little wine) to allow the flavours to fully develop in this delicious French classic: definitely one for the repertoire.

SERVES 6 **PREP** 20 mins **COOK** 8 hours 30 mins

500ml (2 cups) Burgundian pinot noir
1½ tbs extra virgin olive oil
200g speck or streaky bacon,
   rind removed, cut into batons
500g French shallots, peeled
1 large carrot, peeled, thickly sliced
2 garlic cloves, thinly sliced
1.5kg chuck steak or gravy beef,
   fat trimmed, cut into 5cm pieces
2 tbs plain flour
125ml (½ cup) no-added-salt
   beef stock
200g small Swiss brown mushrooms
1 bunch baby carrots,
   trimmed, peeled
Creamy mashed potato (optional),
   to serve
BOUQUET GARNI
10cm celery stick
5 fresh thyme sprigs
2 fresh continental parsley sprigs
2 fresh bay leaves

1 Bring the wine to the boil in a saucepan over medium-high heat. Reduce heat to medium. Simmer for 5 minutes. Set aside until required.

2 Heat the oil in a large non-stick frying pan over medium heat. Cook the speck, stirring occasionally, for 4 minutes or until golden. Use a slotted spoon to transfer to the slow cooker. Add the shallots and carrot to the pan. Cook, stirring occasionally, for 3 minutes or until golden. Stir in the garlic for 1 minute or until aromatic. Use a slotted spoon to transfer to the slow cooker, reserving fat in pan.

3 Season beef. Return pan to medium-high heat. Cook the beef, in 3 batches, turning, for 4 minutes or until browned. Return all the beef to the pan. Sprinkle with flour. Cook, stirring, for 1 minute or until coated. Add the wine and stock. Cook, stirring, for 4 minutes or until mixture comes to a simmer.

4 To make the bouquet garni, tie the ingredients together with kitchen string. Add to the slow cooker. Cover and cook on Low for 8 hours, adding the mushrooms and baby carrots for the final 2 hours of cooking. Serve with creamy mashed potato, if using.

NUTRITION (PER SERVE)

CALS	FAT	SAT FAT	PROTEIN	CARBS
546	27g	10g	51g	8g

● FREEZABLE ○ GLUTEN FREE ● MAKE AHEAD ○ ONE POT ○ VEGAN ○ VEGO ○ YEAR-ROUND FAVE

★★★★★ This is so delicious. It takes a while
to prepare, but the slow cooker does the rest. **CHARLOTTE73**

CHICKEN AND CHORIZO

GUMBO

Comfort food at its best, this rich and hearty
Cajun-style meal is a definite crowd-pleaser.

SERVES 6 **PREP** 15 mins **COOK** 5 hours 15 mins

1 tsp olive oil

6 chicken thigh cutlets,
  skinless, trimmed

2 chorizo sausages, thinly sliced

1 brown onion, coarsely chopped

1 red capsicum, chopped

1 green capsicum, chopped

1 celery stick, sliced

1 garlic clove, finely chopped

1 tbs plain flour

500ml (2 cups) chicken stock

400g can chopped tomatoes

1 tsp dried thyme

Large pinch of cayenne pepper

150g okra, trimmed, thickly sliced
  diagonally

2 corncobs, kernels removed

65g (⅓ cup) medium-grain white rice

Chopped fresh continental parsley
  leaves, to serve

1 Heat oil in a large non-stick frying pan over medium-high heat. Add chicken. Cook for 3 minutes each side or until just golden. Transfer to the slow cooker.

2 Add the chorizo to frying pan. Cook for 1 minute each side. Add to the slow cooker. Add the onion, capsicum, celery and garlic to frying pan. Cook, stirring often, for 5 minutes or until softened. Add the flour. Cook, stirring, for 1 minute. Add the stock, tomato, thyme and cayenne pepper. Stir to combine. Transfer to the slow cooker.

3 Cover with lid. Cook on Low for 4 hours (or on High for 2 hours). Stir in okra, corn and rice. Cook, uncovered, on Low for a further 1 hour or until chicken and rice are tender. Season. Sprinkle with parsley to serve.

COOK'S NOTE

If you like your food with a little heat, increase cayenne pepper to ¼ tsp.

NUTRITION (PER SERVE)

CALS	FAT	SAT FAT	PROTEIN	CARBS
411	17g	5g	40g	24g

● FREEZABLE ○ GLUTEN FREE ● MAKE AHEAD ○ ONE POT ○ VEGAN ○ VEGO ● YEAR-ROUND FAVE

★★★★★

I thought this was great. I don't normally cook things in the slow cooker that I have to prep first but this was totally worth it. The flavour was fantastic. **TRACEYHOP**

SICILIAN POT ROAST WITH VEAL

The salty tang of the anchovies and the sweetness of the currants make this distinctive Sicilian dish memorable and perfect for weekends.

SERVES 6 **PREP** 20 mins **COOK** 5 hours 15 mins

1 tsp extra virgin olive oil
1kg veal rump roast
1 brown onion, halved, thinly sliced
2 carrots, sliced
2 celery stalks, roughly chopped
2 garlic cloves, thinly sliced
125ml (½ cup) dry white wine
2 x 400g cans diced tomatoes
45g can anchovies, drained
1 cinnamon stick
Pinch of dried chilli flakes
80g (½ cup) currants
80g (½ cup) pitted black olives
2 tbs pine nuts, toasted
Fresh continental parsley leaves
    and couscous, to serve

1 Heat oil in a large deep non-stick frying pan over medium-high heat. Season veal. Add veal to pan. Cook, turning occasionally, for 8 minutes or until browned all over. Transfer to the slow cooker.

2 Reduce heat to medium. Add onion, carrot and celery. Cook, stirring often, for 5 minutes or until softened. Add garlic. Cook for 1 minute or until fragrant. Add wine. Cook for 1 minute. Add tomato, anchovies, cinnamon and dried chilli. Season. Pour over veal. Cover with lid. Cook on Low for 3 hours. Sprinkle with currants. Cover. Cook for a further 2 hours or until veal is tender.

3 Slice veal. Scatter with olives, pine nuts and parsley. Serve with couscous.

COOK'S NOTE

Don't worry that the anchovies aren't chopped; they will dissolve into the sauce, adding a savoury, but not fishy, flavour.

NUTRITION (PER SERVE)

CALS	FAT	SAT FAT	PROTEIN	CARBS
527	11g	3g	43g	55g

★ ★ ★ ★ ★

What a delightful surprise at the end of the day in your slow cooker! I used rump, because that's all I had, but it did not fail to impress the family. **BRAKEITLIKEBEC**

○ FREEZABLE ● GLUTEN FREE ● MAKE AHEAD ○ ONE POT ○ VEGAN ○ VEGO ○ YEAR-ROUND FAVE

SLOW-COOKER BEEF DAUBE

Originally from the Provence region of France, beef daube is a classic winter favourite for good reason. Try this modern, easier version.

SERVES 4 **PREP** 10 mins **COOK** 8 hours 10 mins

2 tsp olive oil
600g beef chuck steak, trimmed, cut into 3cm pieces
1 brown onion, chopped
1 carrot, chopped
1 celery stick, chopped
2 garlic cloves, finely chopped
375ml (1½ cups) red wine
3 tomatoes, chopped
3 fresh thyme sprigs
7cm strip orange rind
2 dried bay leaves
Mashed potato and steamed green beans, to serve

1 Heat half the oil in a large frying pan over medium-high heat. Add beef. Cook, turning occasionally, for 5 minutes or until browned. Transfer to the bowl of a slow cooker.

2 Heat remaining oil in pan over medium heat. Add onion, carrot, celery and garlic. Cook, stirring occasionally, for 5 minutes or until softened. Transfer to the slow cooker.

3 Add wine, tomato, thyme, orange rind and bay leaves to slow cooker. Stir to combine. Cover with lid. Cook on Low for 6-8 hours (or on High for 4 hours), removing the lid halfway through cooking.

4 Remove and discard thyme, orange rind and bay leaves. Season. Serve with mashed potato and green beans.

COOK'S NOTE

Daube is also delicious made with a lamb shoulder.

NUTRITION (PER SERVE)

CALS	FAT	SAT FAT	PROTEIN	CARBS
493	17g	7g	38g	24g

● FREEZABLE ● GLUTEN FREE ● MAKE AHEAD ○ ONE POT ○ VEGAN ○ VEGO ○ YEAR-ROUND FAVE

★★★★★

Tastiest beef dish we've had in years. Made it for the first time when having visitors; everyone loved it and came back for more. I served it with mashed potato and sweet potato and freshly cooked beans. Delicious.

JELLYBABY2

10 mins prep

CURRIES

FROM FIERY TO MILD, SLOW COOKING ALLOWS THESE
AROMATIC CURRIES TO DEVELOP FULLER FLAVOURS.

CHICKEN CURRY WITH MANGO

Using budget-friendly chicken thighs, mango and coconut cream, this aromatic chicken curry is both easy and delicious.

SERVES 4 **PREP** 15 mins **COOK** 4 hours

2 tbs yellow curry paste
1 tsp ground turmeric
6 chicken thigh fillets, trimmed, halved crossways
500g pkt frozen mango cheeks, thawed, coarsely chopped (see note)
2 red capsicum, deseeded, thickly sliced
1 large red onion, cut into wedges
1 tbs finely grated fresh ginger
3 garlic cloves, crushed
1 tbs olive oil
200ml coconut cream
1 tbs brown sugar
2 green shallots, thinly sliced
⅔ cup fresh coriander leaves
1 fresh long red chilli, thinly sliced
Lime wedges and steamed rice, to serve

1 Combine the curry paste and turmeric in a large bowl. Add the chicken, season and toss well to combine. Set aside.

2 Place half the mango in a food processor and process until smooth. Transfer mixture to the bowl of a slow cooker. Stir in 80ml (⅓ cup) water. Top with capsicum, onion, ginger and garlic.

3 Heat oil in a large frying pan over medium-high heat. Add chicken and cook, turning, for 5 minutes or until golden brown. Add to the slow cooker bowl. Cover and cook on Low for 3 hours or until the chicken is starting to become tender.

4 Add coconut cream to the slow cooker. Cover and cook on High for 1 hour or until the sauce thickens slightly. Stir in the remaining mango along with the sugar. Cook for a further 10 minutes or until the mango has warmed through. Turn off slow cooker and set aside for 5 minutes to rest.

5 Sprinkle with green shallot, coriander and chilli. Serve with lime wedges and rice.

NUTRITION (PER SERVE)

CALS	FAT	SAT FAT	PROTEIN	CARBS
867	31g	14g	52g	93g

★★★★★ *An easy winter meal, deliciously balanced.* **POLRENA**

● FREEZABLE ○ GLUTEN FREE ● MAKE AHEAD ○ ONE POT ○ VEGAN ○ VEGO ● YEAR-ROUND FAVE

SLOW-COOKED MAVROU

This South African style of Malay curry is traditionally served at weddings, but also makes a fabulous winter family meal.

SERVES 4 **PREP** 15 mins (+ marinating) **COOK** 8 hours 10 mins

4 cardamom pods, bruised

3 tsp sweet paprika

2 tsp ground coriander

1 tsp cayenne pepper

1 tsp ground turmeric

1 tsp ground cumin

¼ tsp ground allspice

1 cinnamon stick

1.2kg gravy beef, fat trimmed, cut into 4cm pieces

4cm piece fresh ginger, peeled, finely chopped

3 garlic cloves, finely chopped

1½ tbs grapeseed oil

1 brown onion, coarsely chopped

250ml (1 cup) chicken stock

250ml (1 cup) crushed tomatoes

Baby herbs, to serve

Saffron rice, to serve

1 Combine the cardamom, paprika, coriander, cayenne pepper, turmeric, cumin, allspice and cinnamon in a glass bowl. Add beef, ginger and garlic and stir to combine. Season. Cover and place in fridge for 1 hour to marinate (see Cook's Note).

2 Heat the oil in a large non-stick frying pan over medium heat. Cook onion for 5 minutes or until light golden. Stir in beef mixture for 5 minutes or until browned. Transfer to the slow cooker.

3 Put stock, tomato and 125ml (½ cup) water in the same pan. Bring to the boil, then carefully pour over the beef mixture in the slow cooker.

4 Cover and cook on Low for 8 hours or until beef is almost tender. Sprinkle mavrou with herbs and serve with rice.

COOK'S NOTE

Marinate beef for at least one hour, but you can leave it for up to 8 hours if you prefer.

NUTRITION (PER SERVE)

CALS	FAT	SAT FAT	PROTEIN	CARBS
705	20g	5g	60g	68g

Secret Hack

Time hack! When the mavrou is ready, heat up a packet of microwave rice and you're good to go.

○ FREEZABLE ○ GLUTEN FREE ● MAKE AHEAD ○ ONE POT ○ VEGAN ○ VEGO ● YEAR-ROUND FAVE

EASIEST-EVER SATAY PORK

With just 15 minutes of meal prep required, the sauce is super creamy thanks to the coconut milk and peanut butter.

SERVES 6 **PREP** 15 mins **COOK** 6 hours 10 mins

1 tbs olive oil
1.5kg piece pork scotch fillet, trimmed, cut into 4-5cm pieces
1 brown onion, cut into thin wedges
2 garlic cloves, crushed
2 tsp finely grated ginger
90g (⅓ cup) natural crunchy peanut butter
160ml can coconut milk
125ml (½ cup) chicken stock
60ml (¼ cup) light soy sauce
1 tbs sweet chilli sauce
1 red capsicum, deseeded, thinly sliced
2 tbs coarsely chopped unsalted peanuts
Fresh coriander leaves (optional)
Steamed rice, to serve
Lime wedges, to serve

1 Heat the oil in a large non-stick frying pan over medium-high heat. Add one-third of the pork and cook, turning occasionally, for 5 minutes or until golden. Transfer to the slow cooker. Repeat in 2 more batches.

2 Reduce the heat on the stovetop to medium-low. Add the onion and cook, stirring occasionally, for 4 minutes or until softened. Add the garlic and ginger and cook, stirring, for 1 minute or until aromatic. Stir in the peanut butter, coconut milk, chicken stock, soy sauce and sweet chilli sauce. Pour over the pork.

3 Cover and cook on Low for 6 hours or until the pork is very tender. Taste and add a little more sweet chilli sauce if desired. Top with the capsicum, peanuts and coriander, if using. Serve with rice and lime wedges.

COOK'S NOTE

This recipe is just as delicious made with chuck steak or even lamb shoulder.

NUTRITION (PER SERVE)

CALS	FAT	SAT FAT	PROTEIN	CARBS
729	21g	7g	58g	70g

★★★★★ *I really enjoyed this dish. I wouldn't normally choose pork with satay but will be definitely making it again, especially as it was a winner with my son.* **GOZZAJACQ**

● FREEZABLE ○ GLUTEN FREE ● MAKE AHEAD ○ ONE POT ○ VEGAN ○ VEGO ○ YEAR-ROUND FAVE

MASSAMAN BEEF AND POTATO

This oh-so-easy Thai curry tastes authentic, so don't let anyone know you cheated with an off-the-shelf paste. Serve with steamed rice.

SERVES 4 **PREP** 15 mins **COOK** 8 hours 30 mins

1 tbs peanut oil
750g beef chuck steak, trimmed, cut into 3cm cubes
1 medium brown onion, halved, thinly sliced
60g (¼ cup) Thai massaman curry paste
2 garlic cloves, crushed
6 cardamom pods, bruised
1 cinnamon stick
2 kaffir lime leaves, vein removed, chopped
270ml can coconut milk
500g desiree potatoes, peeled, cut into 3cm pieces
2 large carrots, peeled, thickly sliced
60ml (¼ cup) fish sauce
1 tbs palm sugar
1 tbs fresh lime juice
Steamed rice, chopped dry-roasted peanuts and coriander leaves, to serve

1 Heat half the oil in a large frying pan over medium-high heat. Cook beef, in batches, for 5-6 minutes or until browned. Transfer to the slow cooker.

2 Heat remaining oil in pan. Add onion. Cook, stirring, for 5 minutes or until softened. Add paste and garlic. Cook for 1 minute or until fragrant. Transfer to the slow cooker. Add cardamom, cinnamon, lime leaves, coconut milk, potato, carrot, fish sauce and sugar. Cover and cook on Low for 8 hours or until beef is tender.

3 Discard cardamom pods and cinnamon. Add lime juice. Serve with rice and scatter peanuts and coriander over.

COOK'S NOTE

For a change, you could make this with chicken thigh cutlets. Cook on Low for 6 hours.

NUTRITION (PER SERVE)

CALS	FAT	SAT FAT	PROTEIN	CARBS
844	34g	18g	52g	77g

● FREEZABLE ○ GLUTEN FREE ● MAKE AHEAD ○ ONE POT ○ VEGAN ○ VEGO ○ YEAR-ROUND FAVE

★★★★★ *I have made this recipe several times now and it is a winner every time! The only addition I make when cooking the recipe is at stage two where I add two sliced/diced red chillies when I add the onion to the pan for sautéing.* **JAZMYN93**

CAULIFLOWER KORMA

Loaded with authentic Indian spices, this recipe uses a whole cauliflower for extra show-stopping appeal.

SERVES 4 **PREP** 10 mins **COOK** 5 hours 10 mins

500ml (2 cups) vegetable stock
125ml (½ cup) passata
60g (¼ cup) korma curry paste
1.1kg cauliflower, outer leaves removed, base trimmed
90g (⅓ cup) Greek-style yoghurt, plus extra, to serve
60ml (¼ cup) pouring cream
2 tsp cornflour
1 ripe tomato, deseeded, finely chopped
Fresh long green chilli, sliced, to serve
Fresh coriander sprigs, to serve
Flaked almonds, toasted, to serve
Roti (optional), to serve

1 Whisk together the stock, passata and korma paste in the slow cooker. Place the cauliflower upside down in the mixture and turn to coat. Stand upright and cover. Cook on Low for 5 hours or until the cauliflower is tender.

2 Baste the cauliflower with the liquid in the slow cooker. Combine the yoghurt, cream and cornflour in a small jug. Add to the liquid in the slow cooker and stir to combine. Cook for a further 10 minutes or until the sauce thickens.

3 Top cauliflower with the extra yoghurt and scatter with the tomato, chilli, coriander and almonds. Serve with roti, if using.

COOK'S NOTE

This is a great side dish, but you could add a can of drained chickpeas to make a more filling meal.

NUTRITION (PER SERVE)

CALS	FAT	SAT FAT	PROTEIN	CARBS
261	6g	1g	34g	13g

Secret Hack
Make it gluten-free! Check the ingredients of the stock and curry paste, and omit the roti if you want to serve a gluten-free meal.

○ FREEZABLE   ○ GLUTEN FREE   ● MAKE AHEAD   ● ONE POT   ○ VEGAN   ● VEGO   ○ YEAR-ROUND FAVE

NYONYA CHICKEN CURRY

This flavour-packed and aromatic Malaysian curry is the perfect comfort food for entertaining or a simple family meal.

SERVES 4 **PREP** 20 mins **COOK** 4 hours 15 mins

1 tbs vegetable oil
8 small skinless chicken thigh cutlets
1 brown onion, halved, cut into thin wedges
185g jar Malaysian Nyonya curry paste
270ml can coconut milk
125ml (½ cup) chicken stock
1 lemongrass stem, trimmed, bruised
1 cinnamon stick
1 star anise
2 kaffir lime leaves, torn
500g desiree potatoes, peeled, halved
300g cauliflower, cut into florets
2 tsp brown sugar
2 tsp fish sauce
4 roti, warmed
2 cups steamed jasmine rice
Fresh coriander leaves and sliced fresh long red chilli, to serve

1 Heat oil in a non-stick frying pan over medium-high heat. Add chicken. Cook for 3 minutes each side or until browned. Transfer to the slow cooker.

2 Reduce heat to medium. Cook onion, stirring, for 5 minutes or until softened. Add curry paste. Cook for 1 minute or until fragrant. Add coconut milk, stock, lemongrass, cinnamon, star anise and lime leaves. Stir to combine.

3 Transfer mixture to the slow cooker. Top with potato and cauliflower (do not stir). Cover with the lid. Cook on Low for 4 hours or until chicken is tender.

4 Stir in the sugar and fish sauce. Discard lemongrass, cinnamon and lime leaves. Serve with the roti and rice, scattered with coriander leaves and chilli.

NUTRITION (PER SERVE)

CALS	FAT	SAT FAT	PROTEIN	CARBS
1140	69g	26g	51g	74g

COOK'S NOTE

Roti is an Indian-style flatbread, similar to naan, but thinner. Substitute with naan if you can't find roti.

● FREEZABLE ○ GLUTEN FREE ● MAKE AHEAD ○ ONE POT ○ VEGAN ○ VEGO ● YEAR-ROUND FAVE

20
mins prep

145

COCONUT BEEF CURRY WITH PUMPKIN

Allow the rich Indian flavours of this dish to develop while you are out and enjoy the sensation of returning to a spice-filled home.

SERVES 6 **PREP** 10 mins **COOK** 6 hours 20 mins

1 tbs peanut oil
1 tbs finely chopped fresh ginger
80g (⅓ cup) rogan josh curry paste
1.5kg beef chuck steak, trimmed, cut into 4cm pieces
400g can chopped tomatoes
250ml (1 cup) chicken stock
1 sprig fresh curry leaves, plus extra, to serve
600g peeled, deseeded pumpkin, cut into 3cm pieces
1 tbs cornflour
270ml can coconut cream
Steamed rice, to serve

1 Heat the oil in a large saucepan over high heat. Add the ginger and cook, stirring, for 1 minute or until softened. Add the curry paste and cook, stirring, for 1 minute or until aromatic. Add the beef and cook, stirring, for 5 minutes or until well coated.

2 Transfer the beef mixture to the bowl of a slow cooker. Add the tomato and stock. Stir to combine. Add the curry leaves. Cover and cook on High for 5 hours or until the beef is tender. Add the pumpkin. Cover and cook for a further hour or until pumpkin and beef are tender.

3 Place the cornflour and 80ml (⅓ cup) coconut cream in a small bowl and stir to combine. Add to the slow cooker and cook, with the lid removed, for 10 minutes or until thickened.

4 Divide the curry among serving plates. Drizzle with some of the remaining coconut cream (see note). Serve with rice, topped with extra curry leaves.

COOK'S NOTE

Pour any remaining coconut cream into a small plastic container and cover with a lid. Use within 4 days or freeze for up to 3 months.

NUTRITION (PER SERVE)

CALS	FAT	SAT FAT	PROTEIN	CARBS
678	32g	15g	51g	44g

● FREEZABLE ○ GLUTEN FREE ● MAKE AHEAD ○ ONE POT ○ VEGAN ○ VEGO ○ YEAR-ROUND FAVE

★ ★ ★ ★ ★

This recipe is easy to make, had lots of flavour and was very filling served with rice and some green beans on the side. It made heaps so I've frozen the leftovers to use for an easy dinner another night. **LIZ2018**

VEGIE CURRY WITH CHICKPEAS

This healthy creamy curry is slow cooked to perfection. Enjoy for dinner tonight and have the leftovers for lunch later in the week.

SERVES 6   **PREP** 15 mins   **COOK** 3 hours 50 mins

2 tsp vegetable oil
2 tbs Madras curry paste
250ml (1 cup) vegetable stock
400ml can light coconut cream
1 large red capsicum, cut into 2cm pieces
1kg pumpkin, cut into 2cm pieces
1 small cauliflower, trimmed, cut into florets
3 tomatoes, coarsely chopped
300g green beans, trimmed, halved
400g can chickpeas, rinsed, drained
1 Lebanese cucumber, grated
2 tbs chopped fresh coriander leaves, plus extra to serve
260g (1 cup) plain Greek-style yoghurt
4 naan bread, warmed

1 Heat oil in a medium saucepan over medium heat. Add curry paste. Cook, stirring, for 30 seconds or until fragrant. Add stock. Bring to a simmer. Transfer to the slow cooker.

2 Add coconut cream, capsicum and pumpkin to slow cooker. Season. Cover with the lid and cook on Low for 3 hours (or High for 1 hour 30 minutes). Add cauliflower and tomato. Cook for 15 minutes. Add beans and chickpeas. Cook for a further 30 minutes or until beans are just tender.

3 Combine cucumber, coriander and yoghurt in a bowl. Serve curry with naan bread, yoghurt mixture and extra coriander leaves.

COOK'S NOTE

If you have leftovers, they will reheat beautifully for lunch the next day!

NUTRITION (PER SERVE)

CALS	FAT	SAT FAT	PROTEIN	CARBS
663	25g	14g	21g	87g

I've made this recipe a couple of times now and both times myself, my hubby and 2yo loved it... the veg selection is also very adaptable – you could easily substitute things like broccoli, snow peas or sweet potato instead of cauliflower, green beans and pumpkin. **NAT_D**

● FREEZABLE   ○ GLUTEN FREE   ● MAKE AHEAD   ○ ONE POT   ○ VEGAN   ● VEGO   ● YEAR-ROUND FAVE

15
mins prep

CAMBODIAN CURRY WITH COCONUT

This creamy red curry takes inspiration from south-east Asia to create a wonderfully warming winter meal.

SERVES 4   **PREP** 5 mins   **COOK** 6 hours

1½ tbs red curry paste
½ tsp ground turmeric
270ml can coconut milk
900g chicken thigh fillets, fat trimmed, quartered
1 lemongrass stem, white part bruised
5 cardamom pods, crushed
2 kaffir lime leaves
2 tbs desiccated coconut
1 tbs brown sugar
Steamed rice, fresh basil leaves, lime slices, thinly sliced red chilli, to serve

1 Whisk together the curry paste, turmeric and half of the coconut milk in the bowl of a slow cooker. Add the chicken and toss to coat. Add the lemongrass, cardamom, lime leaves and remaining coconut milk. Stir to combine. Cover and cook on Low for 6 hours or until the chicken is very tender.

2 Remove and discard the lemongrass. Stir the desiccated coconut and sugar through the curry. Serve with steamed rice and top with basil, lime slices and chilli.

COOK'S NOTE

You could make this recipe with diced beef instead, for a change.

NUTRITION (PER SERVE)

CALS	FAT	SAT FAT	PROTEIN	CARBS
622	22g	13g	40g	63g

★★★★★ *My children love this curry. I swap the red curry paste for massaman and add chopped red potatoes. It's lovely and creamy and the chicken is so tender.* **AMBER72**

○ FREEZABLE   ○ GLUTEN FREE   ● MAKE AHEAD   ● ONE POT   ○ VEGAN   ○ VEGO   ● YEAR-ROUND FAVE

SWEET POTATO CURRY WITH BEEF

With just 10 minutes prep and a few Asian ingredient standbys,
you can have this heart-warming curry waiting for you after a long day.

SERVES 4 **PREP** 10 mins **COOK** 6 hours 15 mins

1 tbs vegetable oil
800g beef chuck steak, trimmed,
  cut into 4cm pieces
2 tbs Thai red curry paste
1 lemongrass stem, bruised
400ml can coconut milk
500g sweet potato, peeled, cut into
  4cm pieces
3 kaffir lime leaves, plus extra,
  shredded, to serve
1½ tbs fish sauce
1 tsp finely shaved palm sugar
Fresh coriander leaves, to serve

1 Heat the oil in a large frying pan over medium-high heat. Cook the beef, in batches, for 3-4 minutes or until evenly browned. Transfer the beef to the slow cooker.

2 Remove and discard all but 1 tbs of the liquid from the pan. Place over medium heat and add the curry paste and lemongrass. Cook, stirring, for 2-3 minutes or until aromatic. Add the coconut milk and stir until combined. Pour the curry sauce over the beef. Add the sweet potato and kaffir lime leaves. Stir to combine. Cover and cook on Low for 6 hours or until the beef is very tender.

3 Stir through the fish sauce and palm sugar, adding more of each to taste, if desired. Discard the lemongrass and kaffir lime leaves. Transfer the curry to a serving bowl. Top with coriander leaves and extra kaffir lime leaves.

COOK'S NOTE

You'll find palm sugar in the Asian food section of the supermarket. Alternatively, use light brown sugar instead.

NUTRITION (PER SERVE)

CALS	FAT	SAT FAT	PROTEIN	CARBS
586	35g	20g	44g	22g

Secret Hack

Make it gluten free! Simply check the ingredients of the curry paste and serve it with steamed rice, if you like.

● FREEZABLE ○ GLUTEN FREE ● MAKE AHEAD ○ ONE POT ○ VEGAN ○ VEGO ○ YEAR-ROUND FAVE

10
mins prep

★★★★★

Lemongrass is definitely the hero!! Such a flavoursome dish... **SUSIEQ**

CREAMY BUTTER CHICKEN

This perennial favourite Indian-style dish is super-easy cooked in a slow cooker. Just add your preferred side dishes for a delicious and filling meal.

SERVES 6   **PREP** 10 mins   **COOK** 6 hours 35 mins

40g ghee
1 tbs vegetable oil
1 large brown onion, finely chopped
4cm piece ginger, peeled, finely grated
3 garlic cloves, crushed
1½ tbs ground cumin
1 tbs ground coriander
2 tsp paprika
½ tsp ground turmeric
1.2kg chicken thigh fillets, fat trimmed, cut into 4cm-pieces
260g (1 cup) natural Greek yoghurt, plus extra, to serve
400g can crushed tomatoes
2 tbs tomato paste
1 tbs cornflour
60ml (¼ cup) thickened cream
1 bunch English spinach, trimmed, coarsely chopped
Steamed rice, to serve
Fried shallots, to serve
Toasted flaked almonds, to serve
Baby coriander sprigs, to serve
Pappadums, to serve

1 Heat the ghee and oil in a frying pan over medium heat. Add the onion, ginger and garlic and cook for 4 minutes or until softened. Add cumin, coriander, paprika and turmeric. Cook, stirring, for 1 minute or until aromatic. Transfer the mixture to the slow cooker. Add the chicken, yoghurt, tomato, tomato paste and 125ml (½ cup) water. Cover and cook on Low for 6 hours, or on High for 3 hours.

2 Whisk cornflour and 1½ tbs water in a small bowl. Add the cornflour mixture and cream to the curry. Stir until combined. Cook on High for a further 30 minutes or until mixture is thickened slightly. Stir in the spinach. Turn off the slow cooker and set aside until spinach is wilted. Season.

3 Divide the rice among serving bowls. Top with the butter chicken, extra yoghurt, shallots, almonds and coriander sprigs. Serve with pappadums.

COOK'S NOTE

Try some roasted cauliflower, Bombay potatoes or green beans as a side dish, accompanied by a mango chutney.

NUTRITION (PER SERVE)

CALS	FAT	SAT FAT	PROTEIN	CARBS
566	27g	12g	36g	41g

● FREEZABLE   ○ GLUTEN FREE   ● MAKE AHEAD   ○ ONE POT   ○ VEGAN   ○ VEGO   ● YEAR-ROUND FAVE

★★★★★ *Lovely authentic flavours, easy to make, yes there are lots of ingredients but don't let this put you off! Love that the slow cooker does all the work!* **NAPOLI**

10 mins prep

MASSAMAN LAMB SHANKS

This rich and warming curry includes creamy coconut milk for added flavour and will fill the house with beautiful aromas.

SERVES 4 **PREP** 25 mins **COOK** 7 hours 45 mins

4 French-trimmed lamb shanks
2 tbs plain flour
2 tbs olive oil
650g chat potatoes
1 red onion, halved, thinly sliced
80g (⅓ cup) massaman curry paste
160ml (⅔ cup) pineapple juice
2 tbs lime juice
375ml (1½ cups) chicken stock
3 tsp fish sauce
1 cinnamon stick
55g (⅓ cup) roasted unsalted
  peanuts, chopped
400ml can coconut milk
Steamed rice and coriander leaves,
  to serve

1 Place shanks and flour in a large snap-lock bag. Season. Seal bag. Shake to coat. Heat half the oil in a large frying pan over medium-high heat. Cook shanks, in batches, for 4-5 minutes or until browned all over, adding extra oil if necessary. Transfer to the slow cooker. Add potatoes.

2 Heat remaining oil in pan over medium heat. Add onion. Cook, stirring, for 3 minutes or until softened. Add paste. Cook for 1 minute or until fragrant. Add pineapple juice, lime juice, stock and fish sauce. Bring to the boil.

3 Transfer mixture to slow cooker. Add cinnamon stick. Cover with lid. Cook on Low for 6 hours, turning shanks halfway through cooking. Add peanuts and coconut milk. Cook for 1-1½ hours or until lamb is very tender. Serve with steamed rice and coriander.

COOK'S NOTE

French-trimmed means the end of the bone has been cut and cleaned of meat and sinew.

NUTRITION (PER SERVE)

CALS	FAT	SAT FAT	PROTEIN	CARBS
872	40g	22g	52g	71g

○ FREEZABLE   ○ GLUTEN FREE   ● MAKE AHEAD   ○ ONE POT   ○ VEGAN   ○ VEGO   ○ YEAR-ROUND FAVE

PASTAS

TAKE MIDWEEK DISHES TO THE NEXT LEVEL
WITH RICH AND FLAVOUR-FILLED SAUCES.

EASY HOME-STYLE
LASAGNE

Layers of mince, cheese and tomato sauce meld gently together in the slow cooker, enhancing the flavours of this traditional Italian dish.

SERVES 6 **PREP** 30 mins **COOK** 4 hours 25 mins

1 tbs extra virgin olive oil
1kg pork and veal mince
90g (⅓ cup) tomato paste
125ml (½ cup) red wine
680g jar bolognese pasta sauce
250ml (1 cup) chicken stock
1 tbs dried oregano leaves
600ml ctn pouring cream
3 eggs, lightly whisked
300g (3 cups) coarsely grated three-cheese mix
250g pkt dried lasagne sheets
Fresh curly parsley leaves, to serve

1 Heat the oil in a large frying pan over high heat. Cook the mince, stirring with a wooden spoon to break up any lumps, for 10 minutes or until the mince changes colour. Add the tomato paste. Cook, stirring, for 1 minute to coat. Add the wine. Cook for 1 minute or until the wine evaporates. Add the pasta sauce, stock and oregano. Season. Simmer for 10 minutes or until reduced slightly.

2 Meanwhile, whisk the cream and eggs in a bowl until well combined. Season. Stir in 200g (2 cups) cheese.

3 Grease the base and side of a 3.5L slow cooker. (If you have a larger slow cooker, make fewer layers.) Spread a thin layer of the mince mixture over the base. Cover with a layer of lasagne sheets, breaking the sheets to fit if necessary. Drizzle one-fifth of the cream mixture over the lasagne sheets and top with one-quarter of the remaining mince mixture. Continue layering with remaining lasagne sheets, cream mixture and mince mixture, finishing with a layer of cream mixture. Sprinkle with remaining cheese.

4 Cook on Low for 3 hours 30 minutes to 4 hours or until the lasagne sheets are tender and the liquid is mostly absorbed. Carefully remove the bowl from the slow cooker. Set aside, covered, for 10-15 minutes to rest. Scatter with parsley.

NUTRITION (PER SERVE)

CALS	FAT	SAT FAT	PROTEIN	CARBS
771	49g	27g	47g	33g

● FREEZABLE ○ GLUTEN FREE ● MAKE AHEAD ○ ONE POT ○ VEGAN ○ VEGO ● YEAR-ROUND FAVE

PORK AND VEAL MEATBALL RIGATONI

Use the slow cooker and budget-friendly mince to create the perfect stress-free midweek pasta meal.

SERVES 4 **PREP** 15 mins **COOK** 6 hours 55 mins

750g pork and veal mince
25g (⅓ cup) finely grated pecorino cheese
3 garlic cloves, crushed
2 tbs finely chopped fresh continental parsley leaves
15g (¼ cup) fresh breadcrumbs
1 tbs olive oil
1 brown onion, chopped
2 celery stalks, chopped
2 tbs dry sherry
500g jar tomato passata
2 tsp caster sugar
350g dried rigatoni pasta
Finely grated pecorino cheese and baby rocket leaves, to serve

1 Combine mince, cheese, garlic, parsley and breadcrumbs in a bowl. Roll tablespoons of mixture into balls.

2 Heat oil in a saucepan over medium-high heat. Add onion and celery. Cook, stirring, for 4 minutes or until onion has softened. Add sherry. Cook, stirring, for 1-2 minutes or until reduced by half. Stir in tomato passata, sugar and 1.5L (6 cups) cold water.

3 Transfer mixture to the slow cooker. Add meatballs. Cover. Cook on Low for 6 hours or until meatballs are cooked through. Add pasta. Stir to combine. Cook, covered, for a further 45 minutes or until pasta is tender and sauce thickened. Season. Serve with grated pecorino and rocket.

COOK'S NOTE

1.5 litres might seem like a lot of water, but the pasta will absorb it easily.

NUTRITION (PER SERVE)

CALS	FAT	SAT FAT	PROTEIN	CARBS
763	19g	6g	59g	81g

○ FREEZABLE   ○ GLUTEN FREE   ● MAKE AHEAD   ○ ONE POT   ○ VEGAN   ○ VEGO   ● YEAR-ROUND FAVE

15
mins prep

SPINACH AND RICOTTA CANNELLONI

A touch of basil adds extra flavour to this budget-friendly slow-cooked version of a classic vegetarian crowd-pleaser.

SERVES 4 **PREP** 15 mins **COOK** 4 hours 5 mins

1 tbs olive oil
1 small brown onion, finely chopped
1 garlic clove, crushed
700g btl passata
2 tbs shredded fresh basil leaves
250g pkt frozen chopped spinach, thawed, excess liquid removed
220g fresh ricotta
1 egg, lightly beaten
12 instant dried cannelloni tubes
50g shaved parmesan
120g baby rocket leaves

1 Heat oil in a large frying pan over medium heat. Add the onion and garlic. Stir for 2-3 minutes or until soft. Stir in the passata, basil and 250ml (1 cup) water. Bring to the boil. Season. Remove from heat.

2 Combine the spinach, ricotta and egg in a bowl. Season. Place in a sealable plastic bag. Cut 1 corner off the bag to make a hole. Pipe the spinach mixture into the cannelloni tubes. Transfer to a plate.

3 Place 1 cup of the tomato mixture in the slow cooker. Top with filled cannelloni tubes, in a single layer, and the remaining tomato mixture. Cook, covered, on High for 4 hours or until cooked through and tender. Divide among plates. Top with shaved parmesan and rocket leaves.

COOK'S NOTE

A large slow cooker is best for this recipe, so you can fit the cannelloni in a single layer.

NUTRITION (PER SERVE)

CALS	FAT	SAT FAT	PROTEIN	CARBS
410	18g	8g	21g	42g

Secret Hack

The cannelloni makes a perfect next-day lunch. Store leftovers in a sealed container in the fridge for up to 3 days and reheat in a microwave.

● FREEZABLE ○ GLUTEN FREE ● MAKE AHEAD ○ ONE POT ○ VEGAN ● VEGO ● YEAR-ROUND FAVE

DUCK RAGU WITH PAPPARDELLE

This rich and hearty bowl of pasta uses a slow-cooked, French-inspired duck ragu to warm up a winter night.

SERVES 6 **PREP** 30 mins **COOK** 6 hours 45 mins

1.8kg duck
100g sliced pancetta,
    coarsely chopped
1 small brown onion, finely chopped
1 small celery stick, finely chopped
1 small carrot, peeled, finely chopped
2 garlic cloves, finely chopped
2 dried bay leaves
250ml (1 cup) pinot noir
2 x 400g cans chopped tomatoes
250ml (1 cup) chicken stock
3 large fresh rosemary sprigs
¼ tsp Chinese five spice
110g (⅔ cup) pitted green olives,
    coarsely chopped
Cooked pappardelle pasta, to serve
Shredded parmesan and chopped
    fresh continental parsley, to serve

1 Use kitchen scissors to cut along either side of the duck backbone. Discard the backbone. Remove and discard excess fat. Quarter the duck. Season with salt. Cook the duck, in 2 batches, skin-side down, in a large non-stick frying pan over high heat for 5 minutes or until golden. Turn and cook for 2 minutes. Transfer to a slow cooker. Drain the fat from the dish, reserving 1 tbs.

2 Reduce heat to medium. Cook pancetta, onion, celery, carrot, garlic and bay leaves, stirring occasionally, for 8 minutes or until vegetables are soft. Stir in wine for 1 minute, scraping the pan with a flat-edged wooden spoon to dislodge any bits that have cooked onto the base. Add to the slow cooker, along with the tomato. Top with stock, rosemary and Chinese five spice. Cover and cook, carefully turning duck once or twice, for 6 hours or until duck is tender.

3 Use tongs to transfer duck to a plate. Skim any fat from surface of cooking liquid. Transfer liquid to a saucepan and simmer over medium heat for 20 minutes or until it reduces by one-third.

4 Carefully remove and discard the duck bones. Shred the duck meat. Stir into the sauce with the olives until heated through. Season. Toss with the cooked pasta. Divide among serving bowls and top with the parmesan and parsley.

NUTRITION (PER SERVE)

CALS	FAT	SAT FAT	PROTEIN	CARBS
503	23g	7g	61g	7g

● FREEZABLE ○ GLUTEN FREE ● MAKE AHEAD ○ ONE POT ○ VEGAN ○ VEGO ○ YEAR-ROUND FAVE

★★★★★
Love this recipe, one of our favourites. **KATROB1501**

30
mins prep

167

CHICKEN DIANE WITH FETTUCCINE

This traditional meal has been made even easier in the slow cooker. It's a real winner on all counts, with only 10 minutes of prep time!

SERVES 4 **PREP** 10 mins **COOK** 4 hours 5 mins

8 small chicken thigh cutlets, excess fat trimmed
2 tsp extra virgin olive oil
1 brown onion, finely chopped
2 garlic cloves, finely chopped
2 tbs cornflour
125ml (½ cup) chicken stock
250ml (1 cup) pouring cream
180ml (⅔ cup) passata
1 tbs Worcestershire sauce
1 tbs Dijon mustard
200g button mushrooms, thickly sliced
½ x 375g pkt fresh egg fettuccine
Fresh continental parsley leaves, to serve

1 Heat a large non-stick frying pan over high heat. Season the chicken and place, skin-side down, in the pan. Cook for 3 minutes or until golden. Turn and cook for a further 2 minutes. Transfer to the slow cooker.

2 Drain the rendered fat from the pan and discard. Heat the oil in the frying pan. Reduce heat to medium-low. Add the onion and garlic and cook, stirring often, for 2 minutes or until soft. Add to the slow cooker.

3 Meanwhile, place the cornflour in a large jug and gradually whisk in the stock. Add the cream, passata, Worcestershire sauce and mustard. Add mixture to the slow cooker. Cover and cook on Low for 3 hours 30 minutes. Add the mushroom and cook for a further 20 minutes. Add the pasta and cook for 10 minutes or until tender. Scatter with parsley leaves to serve.

COOK'S NOTE

Make sure you use fresh, not dried, pasta for this or it will absorb too much of the liquid.

NUTRITION (PER SERVE)

CALS	FAT	SAT FAT	PROTEIN	CARBS
931	65g	27g	63g	22g

○ FREEZABLE   ○ GLUTEN FREE   ● MAKE AHEAD   ○ ONE POT   ○ VEGAN   ○ VEGO   ○ YEAR-ROUND FAVE

★★★★★ *Worked a treat. Lovely thick sauce – tasted great – everyone loved it.* **LEED**

10 mins prep

VEGETARIAN LENTIL LASAGNE

The lentils help to make this a filling version of a meat-free lasagne.
Packed with healthy vegies, it's all so much easier in the slow cooker.

SERVES 6 **PREP** 25 mins (+ cooling) **COOK** 4 hours 35 mins

1 tbs extra virgin olive oil
1 brown onion, finely chopped
1 carrot, finely chopped
2 celery sticks, finely chopped
200g Swiss brown mushrooms,
    coarsely chopped
4 garlic cloves, crushed
1 tbs dried Italian herbs
125ml (½ cup) dry red wine
2 x 400g cans lentils, rinsed, drained
2 tbs tomato paste
700g btl passata with basil
250ml (1 cup) vegetable stock
400ml tub sour cream
2 eggs, lightly beaten
100g (1 cup) grated pizza cheese
5 fresh lasagne sheets
800g butternut pumpkin, peeled,
    thinly sliced
2 zucchini, peeled into ribbons
Chopped fresh oregano leaves and
    fresh basil leaves
Salad leaves, to serve

1 Heat oil in a large, deep frying pan over medium-high heat. Cook onion, carrot, celery and mushroom, stirring, for 10 minutes or until onion has softened. Add garlic and dried herbs. Cook for 1 minute or until fragrant. Add wine. Bring to the boil. Boil for 2 minutes or until reduced by half. Add lentils, tomato paste, passata and stock. Bring to the boil. Reduce heat to medium. Simmer for 20 minutes or until thickened. Season. Set aside for 10 minutes to cool.

2 Meanwhile, place sour cream, eggs and half the cheese in a bowl. Stir to combine. Season.

3 Cut 4 x 50cm pieces of baking paper. Place one piece on a flat surface. Spray with oil. Top with a second piece. Repeat to make a second stack. Place stacks on top of each other to form a cross. Press into bowl of a greased 5.5L slow cooker. Trim paper if necessary so it sits about 5cm below rim of bowl.

4 Reserve 80ml (⅓ cup) sour cream mixture. Place 1 lasagne sheet in base of prepared slow cooker, trimming to fit. Spoon a quarter of the lentil mixture over lasagne sheet. Arrange a quarter of the butternut pumpkin and zucchini, slightly overlapping, over top. Drizzle with a quarter of the remaining sour cream mixture. Repeat layers 3 more times. Top with remaining lasagne sheet, trimming to fit. Drizzle with reserved sour cream mixture, spreading to cover top.

5 Sprinkle with remaining cheese and cover with lid. Cook on Low for 4 hours or until lasagne sheets and pumpkin are tender. Turn off slow cooker and stand for 10-30 minutes to firm. Scatter with oregano and basil. Serve with salad.

NUTRITION (PER SERVE)

CALS	FAT	SAT FAT	PROTEIN	CARBS
684	37g	19g	25g	53g

● FREEZABLE ○ GLUTEN FREE ● MAKE AHEAD ○ ONE POT ○ VEGAN ● VEGO ● YEAR-ROUND FAVE

TURKEY FETTUCCINE CACCIATORE

The meaty flavours of turkey add a hearty twist to this classic example of Mediterranean homestyle cuisine.

SERVES 4 **PREP** 10 mins **COOK** 6 hours 40 mins

2 tbs olive oil
2 (1kg) turkey drumsticks
1 brown onion, chopped
2 garlic cloves, finely chopped
1 sprig rosemary
2 tbs tomato paste
2 x 400g cans chopped tomatoes
250ml (1 cup) chicken stock
2 tbs oregano leaves, chopped
2 tbs chopped fresh basil leaves
50g (½ cup) pitted kalamata olives
Cooked fettuccine, to serve

1 Heat half the oil in a large frying pan over medium-high heat. Add turkey. Cook, turning, for 5 minutes or until just browned all over. Transfer to the slow cooker.

2 Heat remaining oil in pan. Add the onion, garlic and rosemary. Cook, stirring, for 3 minutes or until softened. Stir in the tomato paste, chopped tomatoes, stock and oregano. Season with pepper. Pour over turkey. Cover with lid. Cook on Low for 6 hours or until turkey is very tender, turning halfway during cooking.

3 Remove turkey from sauce. Discard skin and bones. Shred meat. Return to sauce. Cook for a further 30 minutes. Stir in basil and olives. Serve with fettuccine.

COOK'S NOTE

You could substitute with 1kg chicken drumsticks if you can't find turkey.

NUTRITION (PER SERVE)

CALS	FAT	SAT FAT	PROTEIN	CARBS
715	23g	5g	46g	75g

★★★★★ *Had friends coming for dinner & needed something easy to cook while running around doing other things. This was fantastic, easy & plentiful.* **GFCDBURGE**

● FREEZABLE ○ GLUTEN FREE ● MAKE AHEAD ○ ONE POT ○ VEGAN ○ VEGO ○ YEAR-ROUND FAVE

SALADS

HERE'S HOW VERSATILE YOUR SLOW COOKER CAN
BE – YOU CAN EVEN USE IT TO MAKE SALADS.

SHREDDED CHICKEN WITH LIME

Served with a zingy chilli lime dressing, this salad with slow-cooked chicken is perfect for lunch or dinner.

SERVES 4 **PREP** 20 mins **COOK** 2 hours 5 mins

500ml (2 cups) chicken stock
1 lemongrass stem, pale section
   only, bruised
3cm piece ginger, peeled, sliced
1 star anise
400g chicken breast fillets
125g rice vermicelli noodles
2 carrots, peeled, cut into noodles
1 Lebanese cucumber, halved
   lengthways, seeds removed,
   thinly sliced
200g red cabbage, finely shredded
3 green shallots, thinly sliced
1 bunch fresh coriander,
   leaves picked
½ bunch fresh mint, leaves picked
2 tbs fried shallots

DRESSING
2 tbs sweet chilli sauce
2 tbs fresh lime juice
2 tsp fish sauce
2 tsp peanut oil

1 Combine the stock, lemongrass, ginger and star anise in the slow cooker. Add the chicken. Cover and cook on High, turning chicken halfway, for 2 hours.

2 Transfer the chicken to a plate to cool. Add noodles to the slow cooker. Use tongs or a fork to turn the noodles a couple of times in the stock to soften them slightly and loosen until they're mostly submerged. Cover and cook on Low for 5 minutes. Use tongs to transfer noodles to a colander to drain. Set aside to cool.

3 Meanwhile, for the dressing, use a whisk to combine the sweet chilli sauce, lime juice, fish sauce and peanut oil in a small bowl.

4 Use 2 forks to shred the chicken. Use kitchen scissors to cut the noodles into shorter lengths. Combine the chicken, noodles, carrot, cucumber, cabbage, shallot, coriander and mint in a large bowl. Drizzle with dressing. Toss to combine. Sprinkle with fried shallots.

COOK'S NOTE

Use a julienne peeler or a spiraliser to cut the carrots into noodles.

NUTRITION (PER SERVE)

CALS	FAT	SAT FAT	PROTEIN	CARBS
326	5g	1g	27g	39g

○ FREEZABLE ○ GLUTEN FREE ● MAKE AHEAD ● ONE POT ○ VEGAN ○ VEGO ● YEAR-ROUND FAVE

MEXICAN SPICED PORK AND SALSA

This meal includes a warm blend of aromatic seasonings for added flavour. The refreshing bean and corn salsa provides contrast.

SERVES 6 **PREP** 20 mins **COOK** 8 hours 30 mins

1.5kg piece pork neck (scotch)
1 tbs grapeseed oil
1 red onion, finely chopped
3 garlic cloves, thinly sliced
1 tbs ground cumin
2 tsp ground coriander
2 tsp smoked paprika
½ tsp dried chilli flakes
1 tsp dried oregano
400g can crushed tomatoes
2 tsp caster sugar
Light sour cream (optional), to serve

SALSA
400g can kidney beans, rinsed, drained
310g can corn kernels, drained
1 large avocado, chopped
1 large red capsicum, chopped
¼ cup chopped fresh coriander leaves
2 tbs lime juice

1 Rub pork all over with 2 tsp oil. Season. Heat a large, non-stick frying pan over medium-high heat. Cook pork, turning, for 8-10 minutes or until browned. Transfer to the slow cooker.

2 Add remaining oil to pan. Add onion. Cook, stirring, for 3-4 minutes or until softened. Add garlic, cumin, coriander, paprika, chilli flakes and oregano. Cook, stirring, for 1 minute or until fragrant. Add tomato, sugar and 125ml (½ cup) cold water. Stir to combine. Pour sauce over pork in the slow cooker and cook on Low for 6-8 hours.

3 Transfer pork to a plate and cover with foil to keep warm. Transfer liquid to a saucepan and simmer, stirring occasionally, for 8-10 minutes or until thickened. Season.

4 Meanwhile, to make the salsa, put all of the ingredients in a large bowl. Season. Toss to combine. Thickly slice pork. Serve with sauce, sour cream (if using) and salad.

COOK'S NOTE

To slow cook on the stovetop, simmer the pork in the sauce over low heat for 3 hours, basting with the sauce every 30 minutes, and turning pork halfway through cooking time.

NUTRITION (PER SERVE)

CALS	FAT	SAT FAT	PROTEIN	CARBS
507	20g	4g	62g	17g

○ FREEZABLE ● GLUTEN FREE ● MAKE AHEAD ○ ONE POT ○ VEGAN ○ VEGO ● YEAR-ROUND FAVE

★★★★★

I made this for a dinner party and it went down very well. The salad goes really well with the pork. **SJMKIRBY**

LENTIL AND BARLEY SALAD

This set-and-forget salad is so easy to pull together and looks amazing! The goat's cheese adds a subtle tang that is beautifully balanced by the beetroot.

SERVES 4 **PREP** 10 mins (+ cooling) **COOK** 3 hours

105g (½ cup) French green lentils, rinsed
55g (¼ cup) pearl barley
250ml (1 cup) vegetable stock
125g (½ cup) beetroot dip
4 radishes, thinly sliced
3 celery sticks, thinly sliced
120g goat's cheese, crumbled
60g baby rocket
½ cup fresh mint leaves
Extra virgin olive oil and white balsamic vinegar, to drizzle

1 Combine the lentils, pearl barley and vegetable stock in the slow cooker. Cover and cook on Low for 3 hours. Transfer to a large bowl and set aside to cool.

2 Smear dip over plates. Top with lentil mixture, radish, celery, goat's cheese, rocket and mint. Drizzle with oil and vinegar.

COOK'S NOTE

To make this vegan, simply use a vegan beetroot dip and omit the goat's cheese.

NUTRITION (PER SERVE)

CALS	FAT	SAT FAT	PROTEIN	CARBS
342	17g	6g	16g	26g

Secret Hack

Make it gluten free! Check the ingredients in the stock and dip and replace the barley with quinoa for an allergy-friendly salad.

○ FREEZABLE   ○ GLUTEN FREE   ● MAKE AHEAD   ● ONE POT   ○ VEGAN   ● VEGO   ● YEAR-ROUND FAVE

QUINOA SALAD WITH CITRUS LAMB

The fruity flavours of the honey and orange sauce add a Middle Eastern element to this dish, accompanied by a cauliflower and quinoa salad.

SERVES 4 **PREP** 15 mins **COOK** 6 hours

125ml (½ cup) orange juice
250ml (1 cup) salt-reduced chicken stock
1 tbs honey
2 tsp finely grated orange rind
2 tsp ground cumin
1 tsp ground cinnamon
1kg butterflied lamb leg

CAULIFLOWER AND QUINOA SALAD
1 cauliflower, cut into florets
2 tbs extra virgin olive oil
1 tsp ground coriander
½ tsp ground cumin
¼ tsp ground cinnamon
Pinch of ground chilli powder
200g (1 cup) quinoa, rinsed
375ml (1½ cups) salt-reduced chicken stock
75g (½ cup) dried cranberries
½ cup fresh coriander leaves

1 Place orange juice and stock in the slow cooker. Combine honey, orange rind, cumin and cinnamon in a bowl. Season. Rub all over lamb. Roll up lamb and use kitchen string to tie at 3cm intervals to secure. Place lamb in the slow cooker. Cover and cook on Low for 6 hours, turning halfway through, or until very tender.

2 Meanwhile, to make salad, preheat the oven to 200°C/180°C fan forced. Line a baking tray with baking paper. Place cauliflower on the tray. Drizzle with half the oil. Roast for 20 minutes or until golden and tender.

3 Heat remaining oil in a heavy-based saucepan over medium-high heat. Add spices. Cook for 1 minute or until fragrant. Add quinoa. Cook, stirring, for 2 minutes. Add stock. Bring to the boil. Reduce heat to low. Cook, covered, for 15 minutes or until tender. Remove from heat. Set aside for 5 minutes to cool.

4 Transfer quinoa to a large bowl. Add cauliflower and cranberries. Season. Toss to combine. Remove and discard string from lamb. Shred meat and serve with salad, topped with coriander.

COOK'S NOTE

Drizzle some of the juices from the slow cooker over shredded meat for extra flavour.

NUTRITION (PER SERVE)

CALS	FAT	SAT FAT	PROTEIN	CARBS
1046	40g	13g	102g	60g

○ FREEZABLE ○ GLUTEN FREE ● MAKE AHEAD ○ ONE POT ○ VEGAN ○ VEGO ● YEAR-ROUND FAVE

15
mins prep

Secret Hack

Double it! Try cooking two butterflied lamb legs at the same time. Store one by wrapping in plastic wrap, then foil. Refrigerate for up to 3 days or freeze for up to 2 months.

CHORIZO SALAD WITH PRAWNS

This warm salad makes a perfect not-too-heavy, not-too-light winter meal, with slow-cooked chickpeas as a base.

SERVES 6 **PREP** 20 mins (+ 10 mins standing) **COOK** 8 hours 15 mins

- 210g (1 cup) dried chickpeas
- 750ml (3 cups) salt-reduced gluten-free chicken stock
- 1 gluten-free chorizo sausage, sliced
- 500g green prawns, peeled, deveined, tails intact
- 1 red capsicum, deseeded, thinly sliced
- 350g mixed cherry tomatoes, halved
- 1 small red onion, thinly sliced crossways
- 2 tbs extra virgin olive oil
- 1½ tbs red wine vinegar
- 1 small radicchio
- ⅓ cup fresh continental parsley leaves

1 Combine the chickpeas and stock in the slow cooker. Cover and cook on Low for 5 hours.

2 Heat a small frying pan over medium heat and cook the chorizo for 1-2 minutes each side, until golden brown. Drain on paper towel. Add chorizo and prawns to slow cooker (lift and replace lid as quickly as possible). Cook on Low for a further 30 minutes.

3 Use a slotted spoon to transfer the chickpeas, prawns and chorizo to a large bowl. Add the capsicum, tomato and onion. Drizzle with oil and vinegar. Season.

4 Separate the radicchio leaves and arrange on a large serving platter. Top with the chickpea mixture and scatter with parsley.

COOK'S NOTE

Any remaining liquid can be frozen to add to a soup.

NUTRITION (PER SERVE)

CALS	FAT	SAT FAT	PROTEIN	CARBS
464	18g	4g	35g	39g

○ FREEZABLE ● **GLUTEN FREE** ● **MAKE AHEAD** ○ ONE POT ○ VEGAN ○ VEGO ● **YEAR-ROUND FAVE**

PORK AND PINEAPPLE
RICE BOWL

An accompaniment of lemongrass and lime rice adds
some unexpected zing to this delicious pork roast.

SERVES 8 **PREP** 20 mins **COOK** 8 hours

2kg boneless pork leg
375ml (1½ cups) pineapple juice
60ml (¼ cup) soy sauce
2 garlic cloves, peeled, halved
2 tbs lime juice, plus extra limes
   to serve
2 tbs fish sauce
2 lemongrass stems, trimmed, halved
2 fresh long red chillies, sliced,
   plus extra thinly sliced to serve
1 tsp sea salt
1 Lebanese cucumber,
   sliced diagonally
1 carrot, cut into long matchsticks
½ cup fresh coriander sprigs

LEMONGRASS AND LIME RICE
400g (2 cups) jasmine rice, rinsed
80ml (⅓ cup) lime juice
2 lemongrass stems, trimmed, halved
2 tsp finely grated lime rind

1 Remove and discard string from pork. Using a sharp knife, carefully remove rind from pork. Place rind on a plate. Refrigerate.

2 Place pork in the slow cooker. Add pineapple juice, soy sauce, garlic, lime juice, fish sauce, lemongrass and chilli. Cover. Cook on Low for 8 hours (or High for 4 hours), turning pork halfway through cooking, or until very tender. Turn slow cooker off.

3 Meanwhile, preheat the oven to 220°C/200°C fan forced. Cut half of the reserved pork rind into 2cm strips. Discard remaining rind. Sprinkle with sea salt. Set aside for 10 minutes. Place rind on a rack set over a baking tray. Roast for 30-35 minutes or until golden and puffed.

4 Meanwhile, to make the lemongrass and lime rice, put the rice, 750ml (3 cups) water, lime juice and lemongrass in a large saucepan over high heat. Bring to the boil. Reduce heat to low. Cover. Simmer gently for 12 minutes or until liquid is absorbed and rice is tender. Remove from heat. Set aside for 5 minutes. Fluff rice with a fork. Stir in the lime zest. Season.

5 Remove pork from cooking liquid. Using two forks, coarsely shred meat. Arrange the pork, rice, cucumber and carrot in serving bowls. Drizzle with cooking liquid. Top with extra chilli, pork crackling and coriander sprigs. Serve with halved or quartered limes.

NUTRITION (PER SERVE)

CALS	FAT	SAT FAT	PROTEIN	CARBS
645	22g	8g	60g	50g

○ FREEZABLE   ○ GLUTEN FREE   ● MAKE AHEAD   ○ ONE POT   ○ VEGAN   ○ VEGO   ● YEAR-ROUND FAVE

LAMB WITH ALMOND AND POMEGRANATE

A hit of tangy sweet pomegranate and some Middle Eastern spices take this delicious lamb roast to the next level.

SERVES 4 **PREP** 15 mins **COOK** 6 hours 10 mins

1 tsp olive oil
1.2kg easy-carve leg of lamb
1 brown onion, thinly sliced
2 garlic cloves, finely chopped
3cm piece fresh ginger, peeled, finely chopped
400g can chopped tomatoes
2 carrots, thickly sliced
1 whole small red chilli
2 tsp ground cumin
Large pinch of saffron threads
95g (½ cup) raisins
Arils of ½ pomegranate
Cooked quinoa, flaked natural almonds, fresh mint leaves, fresh coriander leaves and extra pomegranate arils, to serve

1 Heat oil in a large frying pan over medium-high heat. Add lamb. Cook, turning, for 5 minutes or until browned all over. Transfer to the slow cooker.

2 Reduce heat to medium. Add onion to pan. Cook, stirring, for 5 minutes or until softened. Add garlic and ginger. Cook for 1 minute or until fragrant. Transfer to the slow cooker. Add tomatoes, carrot, chilli, cumin, saffron and 125ml (½ cup) cold water. Stir to combine. Cover with lid.

3 Cook on Low for 6 hours (or on High for 3 hours), adding raisins halfway through cooking. Season. Stir in pomegranate arils.

4 Slice lamb. Serve with quinoa, sprinkled with almonds, mint, coriander and extra pomegranate arils.

COOK'S NOTE

To release pomegranate arils, cut pomegranate in half and submerge in a large bowl of water. Pull apart under water. Arils will sink to the bottom and you will avoid stains.

NUTRITION (PER SERVE)

CALS	FAT	SAT FAT	PROTEIN	CARBS
706	24g	7g	63g	58g

○ FREEZABLE ● GLUTEN FREE ● MAKE AHEAD ○ ONE POT ○ VEGAN ○ VEGO ● YEAR-ROUND FAVE

15
mins prep

★★★★★ This was easy and very tasty. I cooked the lamb 30 minutes less than the time recommended and while it was resting I added couscous to the juices in the slow cooker as a substitute for the quinoa and it was a great hit. Will make again. CLASS

BAKES

VEGIES, FRITTATA, BREAD AND RIBS IN THE SLOW
COOKER? YOU'LL BE DELIGHTED WITH THE RESULTS.

CREAMY VEGETARIAN 'BAKE'

Layered with potato, sweet potato and carrot, this version of a potato bake has a creamy, cheesy sauce for total crowd appeal.

SERVES 4 **PREP** 15 mins **COOK** 4 hours

300ml pouring cream
2 garlic cloves, crushed
1 tsp vegetable stock powder
800g desiree potatoes, washed
400g sweet potato, peeled
2 carrots, peeled, sliced
1 small brown onion, thinly sliced
40g (½ cup) finely grated cheddar
20g (¼ cup) finely grated parmesan
Ground paprika, to sprinkle
Fresh continental parsley leaves,
 to sprinkle

1 Combine the cream, garlic and stock powder in a jug. Slice the potato, sweet potato, carrot and onion into 5-7mm discs. Grease the bowl of a slow cooker with a little olive oil.

2 Layer the vegetables in the slow cooker, drizzling each layer with the cream mixture. Cover and cook on High for 3 hours.

3 Uncover and sprinkle with cheddar and parmesan. Wipe the moisture from the underside of the lid. Lay a clean, dry tea towel over the slow cooker. Cover with the lid and fold the overhanging tea towel up (so it sits on the lid, not hanging down the side of the slow cooker).

4 Continue to cook for 1 hour or until potatoes are tender and cheese melted. Sprinkle with paprika and fresh parsley to serve.

COOK'S NOTE

The tea towel under the lid stops condensation dripping onto the cheese topping.

NUTRITION (PER SERVE)

CALS	FAT	SAT FAT	PROTEIN	CARBS
536	33g	21g	13g	42g

○ FREEZABLE ○ GLUTEN FREE ● **MAKE AHEAD** ● **ONE POT** ○ VEGAN ● **VEGO** ○ YEAR-ROUND FAVE

PORK RIBS WITH SMOKED SPICES

Pop these barbecue ribs in the slow cooker in the morning and come home to sticky, melt-in-your-mouth deliciousness.

SERVES 4 **PREP** 10 mins **COOK** 8 hours 5 mins

1 tbs smoked paprika
1 tbs ground cumin
2 tsp dried oregano
1 tsp garlic powder
125 ml (½ cup) barbecue sauce,
 plus extra to serve
80 ml (⅓ cup) tomato sauce
2 tbs white wine vinegar
80 ml (⅓ cup) golden syrup
2kg American-style pork ribs

1 Combine paprika, cumin, oregano and garlic powder in a bowl. Add sauces, vinegar and golden syrup. Season with salt and pepper.

2 Cut ribs into portions large enough to fit in slow cooker bowl. Layer ribs and sauce mixture in slow cooker bowl, finishing with the sauce mixture. Cover with lid. Cook on Low for 8 hours.

3 Preheat grill on high. Place ribs on a large foil-lined baking tray. Spoon over some of the sauce from the slow cooker. Grill for 3-4 minutes or until ribs start to char and caramelise. Serve ribs with extra barbecue sauce.

COOK'S NOTE

You can add 1-2 tbs of sriracha chilli sauce if you want extra heat with your ribs.

NUTRITION (PER SERVE)

CALS	FAT	SAT FAT	PROTEIN	CARBS
1186	61g	24g	47g	61g

★★★★★ *Amazing!! I've never cooked ribs before but this was so easy and they tasted amazing. Will definitely use this for my next entertaining dinner.* **SAIDDLES**

○ FREEZABLE   ○ GLUTEN FREE   ● **MAKE AHEAD**   ● **ONE POT**   ○ VEGAN   ○ VEGO   ● **YEAR-ROUND FAVE**

CHEESY POTATO WITH FENNEL

The distinctive aniseed flavours of fennel give this creamy slow-cooked potato 'bake' a delicious taste twist.

SERVES 4 (as a side) **PREP** 20 mins **COOK** 3 hours 50 mins

1 small fennel bulb
1 leek, trimmed, thinly sliced
2 large garlic cloves, very finely chopped
1kg coliban potatoes, very thinly sliced
100g (1 cup) grated 3-cheese blend
300ml ctn cooking cream
40g (½ cup) finely grated parmesan
1 small red onion, thinly sliced crossways
¼ cup small fresh continental parsley leaves

1 Trim the fronds from the fennel and reserve. Thinly slice the fennel and transfer to a bowl. Add the leek and garlic. Toss to combine.

2 Lightly grease the slow cooker and line with baking paper. Arrange one-third of the potato, overlapping slightly, in the base of the prepared slow cooker. Top with one-third of the fennel mixture and one-third of the cheese. Drizzle with one-third of the cream. Season.

3 Repeat with 2 more layers of the remaining potato, fennel mixture, cheese and cream. Cover and cook on High for 3 hours 30 minutes or until the potato is tender. Sprinkle with the parmesan, cover and cook for a further 20 minutes or until cheese has melted.

4 Serve topped with the red onion, parsley and reserved fennel fronds.

COOK'S NOTE

Cooking cream is designed so that it will not curdle or split when heated.

NUTRITION (PER SERVE)

CALS	FAT	SAT FAT	PROTEIN	CARBS
564	37g	23g	19g	36g

○ FREEZABLE ● GLUTEN FREE ● MAKE AHEAD ○ ONE POT ○ VEGAN ● VEGO ○ YEAR-ROUND FAVE

RIBS WITH ROSEMARY
CAULIFLOWER

These deliciously rich and sticky ribs are accompanied with a side of cheesy rosemary cauliflower for the ultimate taste combination.

SERVES 4 **PREP** 25 mins **COOK** 6 hours 20 mins

1 tbs olive oil

1.4kg beef short ribs, excess fat trimmed

150g speck, rind removed, cut into strips

4 garlic cloves, thinly sliced

40g (¼ cup) plain flour

2 tbs tomato paste

375ml (1½ cups) red wine

500ml (2 cups) beef stock

2 sprigs fresh rosemary, plus extra to serve

2 dried bay leaves

¼ cup chopped fresh continental parsley

ROSEMARY CAULIFLOWER

½ (about 600g) cauliflower, cut into florets

30g butter

40g (¼ cup) plain flour

500ml (2 cups) milk

2 tsp finely chopped fresh rosemary

60g (¾ cup) finely grated parmesan

White pepper, to season

1 Heat oil in a non-stick frying pan over medium-high heat. Cook ribs, in batches, for 2-3 minutes each side or until golden. Transfer to the slow cooker.

2 Add the speck to the pan. Cook, stirring occasionally, for 5 minutes or until golden. Add the garlic. Cook, stirring, for 1 minute or until aromatic. Add the flour and tomato paste. Cook, stirring, for 1 minute. Slowly add the wine, stirring constantly until smooth.

3 Add stock, rosemary and bay leaves to the speck mixture. Stir to combine then pour over ribs in the slow cooker. Cover and cook on Low for 6 hours.

4 Meanwhile, to make the cauliflower, microwave cauliflower for 4 minutes or until just tender. Transfer to a baking dish. Heat butter in a saucepan over medium heat until foaming. Add flour. Cook, stirring, for 2 minutes or until bubbling. Remove from heat. Slowly add milk, stirring until smooth. Place over medium-high heat. Cook, stirring, for 5 minutes or until boiling and thickened. Remove from heat. Stir in rosemary and half the cheese. Season with salt and white pepper. Preheat grill on high. Pour sauce over cauliflower. Top with remaining cheese. Grill, 10cm from heat, for 5 minutes or until golden. Set aside for 3 minutes.

5 Transfer beef to a serving dish and sprinkle with parsley and extra rosemary. Serve with cauliflower.

NUTRITION (PER SERVE)

CALS	FAT	SAT FAT	PROTEIN	CARBS
712	36g	16g	58g	27g

● FREEZABLE   ○ GLUTEN FREE   ● MAKE AHEAD   ○ ONE POT   ○ VEGAN   ○ VEGO   ○ YEAR-ROUND FAVE

★★★★★
Wonderful. 10/10 from hubby and myself. Super easy in the slow cooker and the cauliflower was also easy as. Will be doing this again. **CUBBYHOUSE**

25
mins prep

199

SLOW-COOKER CHORIZO
FRITTATA

This cheesy frittata is perfect for easy entertaining, or for a relaxed midweek meal. Just set and forget in the slow cooker.

SERVES 6   **PREP** 15 mins   **COOK** 2 hours 35 mins

1 tbs olive oil
½ brown onion, finely chopped
1 chorizo, sliced into rounds
1 small red capsicum, deseeded, coarsely chopped
6 cherry tomatoes, halved
2 tbs fresh continental parsley, chopped, plus extra sprigs, to serve
½ tsp smoked paprika
8 eggs
40g (½ cup) coarsely grated cheddar cheese

1 Lightly grease a 3.5L slow cooker with spray oil. Heat the olive oil in a large frying pan over medium heat. Cook onion and chorizo, stirring often, for 3-4 minutes or until chorizo is golden and caramelised. Transfer to the slow cooker along with the capsicum, cherry tomato and parsley. Sprinkle with the paprika.

2 Whisk together the eggs and cheese. Season. Pour over the chorizo mixture. Cover and cook on Low for 2½ hours or until the egg is set. Scatter extra parsley leaves over to serve.

COOK'S NOTE

Cooking time will vary depending on the capacity of your slow cooker. Bigger slow cookers with a larger surface area will cook more quickly.

NUTRITION (PER SERVE)

CALS	FAT	SAT FAT	PROTEIN	CARBS
196	13g	5g	15g	3g

★★★★★

Really easy. Never made frittata in a slow cooker before and was worried it would affect the texture. But the chorizo really adds flavour and moisture. **VIOLAPARMESAN**

○ FREEZABLE   ○ GLUTEN FREE   ● MAKE AHEAD   ○ ONE POT   ○ VEGAN   ○ VEGO   ● YEAR-ROUND FAVE

MIDDLE EASTERN STUFFED
CAPSICUMS

Stuffed with a combination of rice, currants and passata, these capsicums are great as a main meal or light lunch.

SERVES 4 **PREP** 20 mins **COOK** 4 hours

8 small red, yellow and
  green capsicums
250g pkt microwave brown rice
80ml (⅓ cup) passata
55g (⅓ cup) currants
2 green shallots, thinly sliced
2 tbs extra virgin olive oil
Greek-style yoghurt, fresh coriander
  leaves and pomegranate arils,
  to serve

1 Lightly grease the slow cooker and line with baking paper. Cut the tops off the capsicums and discard. Remove the seeds and membrane. Place the capsicums, cut-side up, in the prepared slow cooker.

2 Combine the rice, passata, currants, shallot and 60ml (¼ cup) water in a bowl. Season well. Divide the mixture among the capsicums. Drizzle with the oil, cover and cook on High for 4 hours or until the capsicums are soft.

3 Transfer the stuffed capsicums to a serving platter and serve topped with yoghurt, coriander and pomegranate.

COOK'S NOTE

You could serve 2 of these as a vegetarian main course with salad, or as a side dish for steak, lamb or chicken.

NUTRITION (PER SERVE)

CALS	FAT	SAT FAT	PROTEIN	CARBS
352	13g	3g	10g	44g

Secret Hack
Make it vegan! Serve with coconut yoghurt instead to create a delicious vegan-friendly meal.

○ FREEZABLE   ○ GLUTEN FREE   ● MAKE AHEAD   ● ONE POT   ○ VEGAN   ● VEGO   ● YEAR-ROUND FAVE

20
mins prep

CHEESY GARLIC
PULL-APART

Who says you can't make bread in a slow cooker?
This deliciously easy recipe will keep the family happy – and full!

MAKES 8 **PREP** 15 mins **COOK** 2 hours 30 mins

170g butter, chopped
375g (2½ cups) plain flour
2 tsp baking powder
1 tsp salt
250ml (1 cup) buttermilk
1 egg, lightly whisked
3 garlic cloves, very finely chopped
2 tbs finely chopped fresh
   continental parsley leaves
2 tbs finely shredded fresh basil
   leaves, plus extra leaves, to serve
55g (½ cup) pre-grated
   3 cheese blend

1 Lightly grease the bowl of a 5.5L slow cooker and line with baking paper. Place the butter in a microwave-safe jug. Microwave on High for 1 minute or until melted.

2 Whisk together the flour, baking powder and salt in a bowl. Make a well in the centre. Add the buttermilk, egg and 125ml (½ cup) melted butter. Use a flat-bladed knife to mix until mixture comes together.

3 Turn the dough onto a lightly floured surface. Knead for 30 seconds or until smooth. Divide into 8 pieces.

4 Add garlic, parsley and basil to remaining melted butter. Place in a shallow bowl. Gently roll a piece of dough into a smooth ball and roll in the garlic mixture to coat. Transfer to prepared slow cooker. Repeat with remaining dough and garlic mixture.

5 Cover and cook on High for 2 hours or until the bread is cooked through. Sprinkle with the cheese, cover and cook for a further 30 minutes or until the cheese is bubbling. Serve sprinkled with extra basil leaves.

COOK'S NOTE

This is delicious served warm alongside your favourite soup.

NUTRITION (PER SERVE)

CALS	FAT	SAT FAT	PROTEIN	CARBS
374	21g	13g	10g	36g

○ FREEZABLE ○ GLUTEN FREE ● MAKE AHEAD ○ ONE POT ○ VEGAN ● VEGO ● YEAR-ROUND FAVE

PICKLED VEG WITH MISO
EGGPLANT

Enjoy the umami flavours of Japan with sushi rice, miso-flavoured eggplant and pickled vegetables – all made easy with the use of a slow cooker.

SERVES 4 **PREP** 20 mins **COOK** 4 hours

80g (¼ cup) white miso paste
2 tsp soy sauce
2 garlic cloves, crushed
½ tsp sesame oil
2 tbs mirin seasoning
2 tsp caster sugar
2 eggplant, halved lengthways
200g (1 cup) sushi rice
Pickled ginger, sliced green shallot and toasted sesame seeds, to serve

PICKLED VEGETABLES
1 small carrot, cut into thin matchsticks
1 small Lebanese cucumber, deseeded, cut into thin matchsticks
80ml (⅓ cup) rice wine vinegar
2 tsp caster sugar

1 Combine miso paste, soy sauce, garlic, oil, mirin, sugar and 2 tbs water in a jug. Spoon 2 tbs miso mixture into the slow cooker, spreading to cover base.

2 Using a sharp knife, score the flesh of the eggplant in a crisscross pattern, being careful not to cut through the skin. Place in slow cooker, cut side up. Spoon remaining miso mixture over. Cook on High for 2 hours (or Low for 4 hours), basting with miso mixture halfway through cooking.

3 Meanwhile, to make the pickled vegetables, place the carrot, cucumber, vinegar, sugar and 2 tbs water in a bowl. Season. Cover. Set aside for 2 hours.

4 Just before the eggplant is ready, rinse rice under cold water. Cook the rice, using absorption method, following packet directions.

5 Drain pickled vegetables. Rinse under cold water. Drain well. Serve eggplant with pickled vegetables, ginger, shallot and rice. Sprinkle with sesame seeds.

COOK'S NOTE
If you like, first sear the eggplant in a lightly oiled frying pan to make them nicely golden brown.

NUTRITION (PER SERVE)

CALS	FAT	SAT FAT	PROTEIN	CARBS
380	3g	0.3g	9g	73g

○ FREEZABLE   ○ GLUTEN FREE   ● MAKE AHEAD   ○ ONE POT   ● VEGAN   ● VEGO   ● YEAR-ROUND FAVE

CABBAGE ROLLS WITH LEMON SAUCE

Served with a creamy sauce, these slow-cooker cabbage rolls are ideal as a light meal or entrée.

SERVES 6 **PREP** 25 mins **COOK** 4 hours 35 mins

1kg mini savoy cabbage
500g pork mince
250g pkt microwave white rice
3 green shallots, sliced
2 tbs chopped fresh dill, plus extra,
  to serve
1 tsp allspice
500ml (2 cups) salt-reduced
  gluten-free chicken stock
1 tbs cornflour
300ml ctn thickened cream
1 tbs fresh lemon juice
Micro herbs, to serve

1. Bring a large saucepan of water to the boil. Add the whole cabbage and cook, turning halfway, for 5 minutes or until lightly blanched. Carefully transfer the cabbage to a colander to drain. Set aside for 5 minutes to cool slightly.

2. Meanwhile, combine the mince, rice, shallot, dill and allspice in a large bowl. Season well.

3. Gently peel away 10 whole leaves from the cabbage. Reserve remaining cabbage for another use. Cut away any thick pieces of core. Slice larger leaves in half crossways.

4. Place about 2 tbs mince mixture on the stem end of a cabbage leaf. Fold in the bottom end and 2 sides and roll up to enclose. Place in a lightly greased slow cooker. Repeat with remaining mince and cabbage leaves. Pour chicken stock over. Cover and cook on Low for 4 hours or until mince is cooked through, cabbage is tender and liquid has almost all been absorbed. Remove rolls and cover with foil to keep warm.

5. Transfer 125ml (½ cup) liquid from the slow cooker to a bowl. Add the cornflour and stir well, then add the cream and lemon juice and stir to combine. Pour into the slow cooker and cook, covered, on High for a further 15 minutes or until the sauce has thickened. Divide cabbage rolls among serving plates. Pour cream sauce over and top with extra dill and micro herbs.

NUTRITION (PER SERVE)

CALS	FAT	SAT FAT	PROTEIN	CARBS
435	29g	16g	21g	22g

○ FREEZABLE ● GLUTEN FREE ● MAKE AHEAD ○ ONE POT ○ VEGAN ○ VEGO ● YEAR-ROUND FAVE

SOUTHERN PORK

RIBS

Keep lots of napkins at the ready, because this fall-off-the-bone recipe is a rich and comforting, finger-licking crowd-pleaser.

SERVES 4 **PREP** 10 mins **COOK** 6 hours 20 mins

1kg pork ribs
1 tsp olive oil
1 brown onion, finely chopped
2 carrots, finely chopped
2 garlic cloves, thinly sliced
400g can diced tomatoes
250ml (1 cup) beer
60ml (¼ cup) barbecue sauce
5 drops Tabasco
Mashed potato, coleslaw and
   corncobs, to serve

1 Cut ribs into portions of 3-4 bones each. Heat the oil in a large, deep non-stick frying pan over medium-high heat. Season pork. Add half the ribs to pan. Cook for 2-3 minutes each side or until browned. Transfer to the slow cooker. Repeat with the remaining ribs.

2 Reduce heat to medium. Add onion and carrot. Cook, stirring often, for 5 minutes or until softened. Add garlic. Cook for 1 minute or until fragrant. Add tomato, beer, barbecue sauce and Tabasco. Stir to combine. Season.

3 Pour over ribs. Cover with lid. Cook on Low for 6 hours or until ribs are tender and falling from the bone. Serve with mashed potato, coleslaw and corn.

COOK'S NOTE

Pork rib racks are often sold as 'Aussie' or 'American-style' pork ribs.

NUTRITION (PER SERVE)

CALS	FAT	SAT FAT	PROTEIN	CARBS
692	37g	13g	30g	51g

★ ★ ★ ★ ★

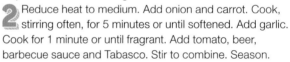

Loved this recipe, so easy! Did a side dish of coleslaw. This was delicious and will definitely make again! **30MARCH1968**

○ FREEZABLE ○ GLUTEN FREE ● MAKE AHEAD ○ ONE POT ○ VEGAN ○ VEGO ● YEAR-ROUND FAVE

DESSERTS

WARM UP TO RICH AND FILLING WINTER PUDDINGS,
CAKES AND BAKES, ALL MADE IN THE SLOW COOKER.

DUMPLINGS WITH SALTED CARAMEL

With a sweet and salty caramel sauce, these golden doughy puffs are perfect for a cosy night in, or end-of-the-meal sweet treat.

SERVES 4 **PREP** 20 mins **COOK** 1 hour 30 minutes

150g (1 cup) self-raising flour
2 tbs caster sugar
40g butter, chilled, chopped
60ml (¼ cup) milk
Large pinch of sea salt flakes
Vanilla ice-cream and custard,
  to serve
CARAMEL SYRUP
185ml (¾ cup) golden syrup
100g (½ cup firmly packed)
  brown sugar
50g butter
185ml (¾ cup) thickened cream

1 Place the lid on the slow cooker and preheat on High while you prepare the dumplings. Combine the flour and sugar in a bowl. Use your fingertips to rub in the butter until mixture resembles coarse breadcrumbs. Make a well in the centre. Add the milk and use a flat-bladed knife to stir until mixture just comes together. Divide into 12 portions and roll gently into balls.

2 For the caramel syrup, combine the golden syrup, sugar, butter, cream and 125ml (½ cup) water in a saucepan over medium-low heat. Cook, stirring, until sugar dissolves and syrup is smooth. Bring to the boil and remove from heat.

3 Pour half the syrup into the preheated slow cooker. Gently place the dumplings in the syrup. Pour the remaining syrup over the top of the dumplings. Cook, covered, for 1 hour 30 minutes or until dumplings are cooked through. Sprinkle with sea salt. Serve with ice-cream and custard.

COOK'S NOTE

These are best served as soon as they are cooked.

NUTRITION (PER SERVE)

CALS	FAT	SAT FAT	PROTEIN	CARBS
891	43g	27g	8g	124g

○ FREEZABLE ○ GLUTEN FREE ● MAKE AHEAD ○ ONE POT ○ VEGAN ○ VEGO ○ YEAR-ROUND FAVE

★ ★ ★ ★ ★

Made this, so good; love it. GREG5464

APPLE CINNAMON
FRENCH TOAST

This set-and-forget twist on a brekky favourite creates an easy dessert, perfect for entertaining or a Saturday night in.

SERVES 4 **PREP** 15 mins **COOK** 3 hours

300g brioche, cut into 2cm pieces
2 Granny Smith apples,
    cored, chopped
140g (1 cup) coarsely
    chopped walnuts
80g (½ cup lightly packed)
    brown sugar
2 tsp ground cinnamon
8 eggs
500ml (2 cups) milk
1 tsp vanilla extract
Icing sugar, to dust
Double cream, to serve
Maple syrup, to drizzle

1 Preheat grill on medium. Place brioche, in a single layer, on a baking tray and grill, turning occasionally, for 4 minutes or until golden.

2 Place the apple, walnut, sugar and cinnamon in a bowl and stir to combine. In a separate bowl, whisk together the eggs, milk and vanilla.

3 Spray a square 17cm, 1.75L (7 cup) glass or ceramic baking dish with oil. Place half the bread in the dish. Sprinkle over half the apple mixture and pour over half the egg mixture. Arrange the remaining bread on top. Sprinkle with remaining apple and egg mixtures.

4 Place a wire trivet or rack in the base of the slow cooker. Put enough warm water into the slow cooker to cover base, leaving top of rack exposed. Place dish on rack. Cook on Low for 2 hours 30 minutes to 3 hours or until just set. Dust with icing sugar and dollop with double cream. Drizzle with maple syrup.

COOK'S NOTE

This recipe would also be delicious with fruit bread, or panettone (Italian Christmas bread).

NUTRITION (PER SERVE)

CALS	FAT	SAT FAT	PROTEIN	CARBS
1014	32g	14g	32g	107g

○ FREEZABLE ○ GLUTEN FREE ● MAKE AHEAD ○ ONE POT ○ VEGAN ○ VEGO ○ YEAR-ROUND FAVE

15
mins prep

Secret Hack
Make it special! Divide the mixture into four individual ramekins for added wow factor when entertaining.

APPLE AND RHUBARB COBBLER

This cinnamon-infused apple and rhubarb cobbler features a soft sponge and plenty of sweet fruit – it really is the perfect winter dessert.

SERVES 6 **PREP** 20 mins **COOK** 3 hours

800g Granny Smith apples, peeled, cored, chopped
1 bunch (about 650g) rhubarb, trimmed, chopped
2 tbs caster sugar
150g (1 cup) self-raising flour
155g (¾ cup firmly packed) brown sugar
Large pinch of ground cinnamon
60g butter, chilled, chopped
1 egg, lightly whisked
2 tbs milk
Icing sugar, to dust
Vanilla ice-cream, to serve

1. Combine apple, rhubarb and sugar in a bowl. Spoon into a 1.5L (6 cup) heatproof dish that fits inside the slow cooker. Place a wire trivet or rack in slow cooker. Put enough warm water into the slow cooker to cover the base, leaving the top of the rack exposed. Place the dish on the rack. Cover with the lid and cook on High for 1 hour 30 minutes.

2. Sift the flour, brown sugar and cinnamon into a large bowl. Use your fingertips to rub in the butter until the mixture resembles coarse breadcrumbs. Make a well in the centre. Whisk the egg and milk in a jug. Pour into the well and use a large metal spoon to gently stir until just combined.

3. Remove the lid from the slow cooker and gently stir the fruit mixture. Drop large spoonfuls of batter over the top of the fruit mixture (don't worry if it's not completely covered). Cover with the lid and cook for a further 1 hour 30 minutes or until the topping is firm to touch and cooked through. Carefully remove the dish from the slow cooker and dust with icing sugar. Serve with scoops of ice-cream.

COOK'S NOTE

Use a dish that's the same shape as your slow cooker, without a lip, and that fits snugly without touching the cooker.

NUTRITION (PER SERVE)

CALS	FAT	SAT FAT	PROTEIN	CARBS
256	12g	2g	11g	23g

○ FREEZABLE   ○ GLUTEN FREE   ● MAKE AHEAD   ● ONE POT   ○ VEGAN   ○ VEGO   ○ YEAR-ROUND FAVE

UPSIDE-DOWN MANDARIN PUDDING

Pop a few ingredients in your slow cooker and come back later to a luscious citrussy winter pudding. It's all so easy!

SERVES 8 **PREP** 20 mins **COOK** 2 hours 30 mins

2 tbs firmly packed brown sugar
3 large mandarins
125g butter, softened
155g (¾ cup) caster sugar
2 eggs, lightly beaten
120g (¾ cup) self-raising flour
85g (¾ cup) almond meal
Double cream and honey, to serve

1 Grease a 6cm-deep, 9cm x 19cm (base) loaf pan. Line base and sides with baking paper, allowing a 2cm overhang. Sprinkle brown sugar over base. Thinly slice 1 mandarin. Arrange slices over sugar. Juice remaining mandarins.

2 Using an electric mixer, beat butter and caster sugar until light and fluffy. Add eggs, one at a time, beating until just combined. Stir in flour, almond meal and 60ml (¼ cup) mandarin juice until just combined.

3 Carefully spoon mixture over mandarin. Smooth top. Place a wire trivet or rack in the base of the slow cooker. Add enough warm water to slow cooker to cover the base, leaving top of rack exposed. Cover with lid. Cook on High for 2 hours 30 minutes or until a skewer inserted in centre comes out clean. Set aside to cool in pan for 5 minutes. Turn onto a plate. Serve warm with cream and honey.

COOK'S NOTE

Replace the mandarins with small oranges, lemons or limes, if you like.

NUTRITION (PER SERVE)

CALS	FAT	SAT FAT	PROTEIN	CARBS
349	20g	9g	6g	36g

★★★★★ *This was absolutely lovely. It has a very subtle citrus flavour, so if you want more of a citrus hit I would suggest increasing the amount of mandarin.* **PENNY86**

○ FREEZABLE   ○ GLUTEN FREE   ● MAKE AHEAD   ● ONE POT   ○ VEGAN   ○ VEGO   ○ YEAR-ROUND FAVE

RASPBERRY

SCROLLS

With just five ingredients, these easy scrolls evoke the classic puddings of last century. They're doughy, fluffy and moist all at the same time.

MAKES 12 **PREP** 20 mins **COOK** 1 hour 45 mins

375g (2½ cups) self-raising flour
60g cold butter, chopped
395g can sweetened condensed milk
115g (⅓ cup) raspberry jam
125g fresh or thawed frozen
   raspberries
Icing sugar, to dust
Vanilla custard, to serve

1 Place the flour and butter in a large bowl. Use your fingertips to rub the butter into the flour until evenly combined. Make a well in the centre. Pour the condensed milk into the centre and use a flat-bladed knife to stir until the mixture starts to come together.

2 Use your hands to press the dough into a rectangle. Roll out on a sheet of baking paper to about 20 x 30cm. Spread dough with the jam and scatter the raspberries over. Starting from a long side, roll up to enclose the raspberries.

3 Cut the log into 12 thick slices (trim off the ends first, to neaten, if you like). Line the slow cooker with a large sheet of baking paper, allowing it to come about halfway up the side. Arrange the scrolls over the base of the slow cooker. Lay a tea towel over the top, then put on the lid. Fold the overhanging tea towel up so it sits on the lid, not hanging down the side of the slow cooker.

4 Cook on High for 1 hour 45 minutes or until the scrolls are lightly golden and cooked through. Use the paper to transfer to a board. Set aside to cool slightly. Dust with icing sugar and serve with custard.

COOK'S NOTE

Substitute lemon curd for the jam for extra tang, if you like.

NUTRITION (EACH)

CALS	FAT	SAT FAT	PROTEIN	CARBS
303	8g	4g	7g	52g

○ FREEZABLE ○ GLUTEN FREE ● MAKE AHEAD ● ONE POT ○ VEGAN ○ VEGO ○ YEAR-ROUND FAVE

CINNAMON AND VANILLA QUINCES

The quintessential winter fruit, these poached quinces are perfect for a crumble, or even to serve with your morning porridge.

SERVES 4 **PREP** 20 mins **COOK** 10 hours

215g (1 cup) caster sugar
1 vanilla bean, split
1 cinnamon stick
1 whole clove
3 (180g each) quinces
Double cream, to serve

1 Place sugar and 1L (4 cups) cold water in a saucepan over low heat. Cook, stirring occasionally, for 5 minutes or until sugar dissolves. Increase heat to medium. Bring to the boil. Remove from heat. Carefully pour sugar syrup into the slow cooker. Add vanilla bean, cinnamon and clove.

2 One at a time, peel, quarter and core quinces and place immediately into sugar syrup (see note). Cover with lid. Cook on Low for 10 hours (or on High for 6 hours) until quince is tender and deep red in colour. Serve quince drizzled with syrup and dolloped with double cream.

COOK'S NOTE

The cut quince will turn brown when exposed to the air, so you will need to work quickly.

NUTRITION (PER SERVE)

CALS	FAT	SAT FAT	PROTEIN	CARBS
370	10g	7g	1g	68g

★★★★★

Yummy. Great with some natural yoghurt and muesli for breakfast, or for dessert with ice-cream. **COOKIESMAMA**

○ FREEZABLE ● GLUTEN FREE ● MAKE AHEAD ○ ONE POT ○ VEGAN ○ VEGO ○ YEAR-ROUND FAVE

Secret Hack
Two-for-one deal! Reserve the poaching syrup and use it to add flavour to sparkling drinks such as mineral water or Prosecco.

HUMMINGBIRD

CAKE

Who said you can't make cakes in a slow cooker? This deliciously rich caramel-and-fruit-laden cake tastes as good as it looks.

SERVES 10 **PREP** 15 mins (+ cooling) **COOK** 3 hours 30 minutes

300g (2 cups) plain flour
200g (1 cup firmly packed) brown sugar
45g (½ cup) desiccated coconut
1 tsp baking powder
1 tsp ground cinnamon
½ tsp bicarbonate of soda
3 eggs, lightly whisked
180ml (¾ cup) light extra virgin olive oil
440g can crushed pineapple
260g (1 cup) mashed banana (about 3 bananas)
105g (¾ cup) pecans, toasted, chopped, plus extra, to serve
Store-bought caramel sauce or dulce de leche, to drizzle

CREAM CHEESE ICING
250g pkt cream cheese, chopped, at room temperature
70g unsalted butter, chopped, at room temperature
1 tsp vanilla extract
300g (2 cups) icing sugar mixture

1 Grease a round 20cm (base measurement) cake pan that fits inside the slow cooker. Line the base of the pan with baking paper. Whisk flour, sugar, coconut, baking powder, cinnamon, bicarb and a pinch of salt in a bowl until combined. Make a well in centre.

2 Add egg, oil, pineapple and banana to the well. Stir to combine. Stir in the pecans. Pour into prepared pan. Smooth surface. Place a wire trivet or rack in the slow cooker. Add enough warm water to slow cooker to cover base, leaving top of rack exposed. Place pan on rack. Cover and cook on Low for 3 hours 30 minutes or until a skewer inserted in centre of cake comes out clean. Remove from the slow cooker and cool completely in pan.

3 For the icing, use an electric beater to beat the cream cheese, butter and vanilla in a bowl until smooth. Gradually beat in the icing sugar until well combined.

4 Use a large serrated knife to cut cake in half horizontally. Spread with a third of the icing. Top with remaining cake. Spread remaining icing all over cake. Drizzle with caramel. Scatter with the extra pecans.

COOK'S NOTE

Decorate with slices of dried pineapple, if you like.

NUTRITION (PER SERVE)

CALS	FAT	SAT FAT	PROTEIN	CARBS
772	43g	14g	9g	87g

○ FREEZABLE ○ GLUTEN FREE ● MAKE AHEAD ● ONE POT ○ VEGAN ○ VEGO ○ YEAR-ROUND FAVE

POACHED RASPBERRY PEARS

Use the best of the winter fruit to create a deliciously satisfying and warming dessert – with minimal prep and only three steps.

SERVES 4 **PREP** 5 mins **COOK** 1 hour 40 mins

70g (⅓ cup) caster sugar
500ml (2 cups) apple, cranberry and raspberry juice
4 medium Packham pears, peeled
1 vanilla bean, split
150g frozen raspberries

1 Combine sugar and juice in a saucepan over medium heat. Cook, stirring, for 5 minutes or until sugar has dissolved.

2 Place pears in the bowl of the slow cooker. Pour syrup over. Add vanilla bean. Cover and cook on High for 1 hour 15 minutes or until pears are almost tender, turning halfway through cooking.

3 Add raspberries. Cook for 15 minutes or until pears are tender. Serve pears with syrup and raspberries.

COOK'S NOTE

Any leftover pears will keep in the fridge for up to 3 days. Serve with cream, if you like.

NUTRITION (PER SERVE)

CALS	FAT	SAT FAT	PROTEIN	CARBS
240	1g	0g	2g	50g

★★★★★ *Alongside the lovely flavours, this dessert is perfect if you have family/friends with gluten intolerance and allergies to egg or dairy.* **RINN**

○ FREEZABLE ● GLUTEN FREE ● MAKE AHEAD ○ ONE POT ● VEGAN ○ VEGO ○ YEAR-ROUND FAVE

GIANT GOLDEN SYRUP DUMPLING

Drenched in a sticky golden syrup sauce, this giant fluffy dumpling is super easy and perfect for entertaining friends and family.

SERVES 6 **PREP** 20 mins **COOK** 2 hours

265g (1¾ cups) self-raising flour
1 tbs caster sugar
½ tsp ground allspice
30g butter
160ml (⅔ cup) milk
1 egg
Vanilla ice-cream, to serve

GOLDEN SYRUP SAUCE

250ml (1 cup) golden syrup
55g (¼ cup firmly packed) brown sugar
1 tsp vanilla extract
50g butter, at room temperature, chopped
500ml (2 cups) boiling water

1. To make the golden syrup sauce, place the golden syrup, brown sugar, vanilla, butter and boiling water in the slow cooker and cover. Set slow cooker to High.

2. Meanwhile, sift the flour, sugar and allspice into a large bowl. Use your fingertips to rub the butter into the mixture until it resembles fine breadcrumbs.

3. In a jug, whisk together the milk and egg. Add to the flour mixture. Use a flat-bladed knife to stir until just combined.

4. Remove the lid from the slow cooker and stir the sauce. Drop large spoonfuls of the dumpling mixture into the sauce (the mixture will join together as it cooks).

5. Lay a clean, dry tea towel over the slow cooker. Wipe the moisture from the underside of the lid, then replace over the tea towel, folding up the overhanging material to sit on the lid. Cook on High for 2 hours or until the dumplings have joined together and are cooked through.

6. Use a large metal spoon to scoop out the dumpling into serving bowls and drizzle with golden syrup sauce. Serve with ice-cream.

COOK'S NOTE

To test if cooked through, insert a toothpick into the centre: if it comes out clean, the dumpling is ready.

NUTRITION (PER SERVE)

CALS	FAT	SAT FAT	PROTEIN	CARBS
572	16g	8g	8g	100g

○ FREEZABLE ○ GLUTEN FREE ● MAKE AHEAD ● ONE POT ○ VEGAN ○ VEGO ○ YEAR-ROUND FAVE

SLOW-BAKED APPLES

Warm and comforting, this recipe is super simple. Fill apples with the sugar 'n' spice filling, then let the slow cooker do all the work.

SERVES 4 **PREP** 15 mins **COOK** 2 hours 30 mins

4 red apples
80g (½ cup lightly packed) brown sugar
45g unsalted butter, at room temperature
2 tbs pecan nuts, finely chopped
2 tbs raisins
¾ tsp ground ginger
Pouring cream, to serve

1 Use an apple corer to core apples, leaving base intact. Use a teaspoon to scoop out the flesh to create a slightly wider cavity. Use a paring knife to score the skin around the circumference of the apples.

2 Combine the sugar, butter, pecan, raisins and ginger in a bowl. Divide among the apple cavities, pushing down well.

3 Place apples in the slow cooker, making sure the apples don't touch the side. Pour 80ml (⅓ cup) water around the apples. Cook on High for 2 hours 30 minutes or until apples are tender. Divide among bowls. Serve with the cream.

COOK'S NOTE

If you don't have an apple corer, use a small sharp knife to remove cores – carefully!

NUTRITION (PER SERVE)

CALS	FAT	SAT FAT	PROTEIN	CARBS
470	31g	18g	2g	49g

These were gorgeous! The hardest part was coring the apples. The great thing about them is that you can put them on and forget about them 'til serving. They look impressive when served in a bowl with a scoop of ice-cream and cream. Yum! **MOTHERBIRD**

○ FREEZABLE ● GLUTEN FREE ● MAKE AHEAD ○ ONE POT ○ VEGAN ● VEGO ○ YEAR-ROUND FAVE

FRESH SIDES

SEASONAL INGREDIENTS MAKE EASY, MOUTHWATERING
SIDE DISHES FOR YOUR SLOW-COOKED MEALS.

These clever ideas for sides make the most of nature's bounty.
Try baked vegies, simple salads and platters of roasted fruits.

baked cabbage

Preheat oven to 200°C/180°C fan forced. Cut red and green baby cabbages into wedges. Drizzle with olive oil. Bake on a lined baking tray until golden. Top with lemon juice and zest, capers and chopped parsley.

green & gold bake

Try this hearty winter vegie side. Preheat oven to 180°C/160°C fan forced. Thinly slice yellow squash and zucchini into rounds. Layer in a baking dish. Drizzle with olive oil. Sprinkle with shredded parmesan and panko breadcrumbs. Bake until golden. Sprinkle with fresh oregano leaves.

cheesy crushed pancetta spuds

Roast whole baby potatoes until just tender, then gently crush with a potato masher. Sprinkle with finely grated parmesan and finely chopped pancetta before roasting for a further 10-15 minutes until crisp.

WINTER WEDGES

Preheat oven to 190°C/170°C fan forced. Cut baby pumpkins into wedges. Drizzle with olive oil. Bake until golden. Top with burnt butter, fried sage leaves, feta and walnuts.

roast apple

When roasting pork, include slow-cooked seasonal fruit for added interest. Cut apples into halves, and add to the slow cooker, along with finely chopped thyme, celery, and brown onion, cooking on the Low setting for 8 hours.

ginger smash

Add some freshly grated ginger and coconut milk to sweet potato mash for a zingy twist!

sweet beets

Roast scrubbed baby beets with orange slices, fresh thyme sprigs, a splash of balsamic vinegar and olive oil and plenty of seasoning in a roasting tray, covered with foil, until tender.

pomegranate topper
Top slow-cooked lamb with a little Greek yoghurt, then sprinkle with a mixture of pomegranate seeds, fresh mint leaves and chopped pistachios.

pumpkin puree
Drizzle halved and deseeded butternut pumpkins with oil. Roast or cook in a slow cooker until tender. Process flesh with a spoonful of coconut cream, grated fresh ginger and chilli flakes until smooth. Make ahead and reheat on the stovetop.

dukkah rainbow carrots
Preheat oven to 190°C/170°C fan forced. Drizzle mixed baby rainbow carrots with oil and sprinkle with thinly sliced garlic. Roast until tender. For an Egyptian flavour twist, sprinkle with pistachio dukkah to serve.

honey grapes
Combine honey, a splash of balsamic vinegar and a little water in the slow cooker. Add seedless red grapes and poach until just soft. Cool, then spoon over a round of brie or with ice-cream.

CORN FLOWERS

Cut steamed corn cobs into 2cm-thick slices. Arrange on a plate. Top with garlic butter, lime zest and finely chopped fresh red chilli.

pear & ham bruschetta

Toss matchsticks of Corella pear in lemon juice, olive oil and a drizzle of honey. Spread toasted sourdough with goat's cheese, then top with ham and the pear mixture.

cider leeks

Sauté rounds of leek in butter until golden brown. Add a good slosh of apple cider and 2 fresh thyme sprigs before simmering for 15-20 minutes, until tender.

pea fry-up

Sauté chopped pancetta, chopped red onion and thinly sliced garlic until golden. Add trimmed, lightly blanched sugar snap peas. Cook until tender crisp. Drizzle with lemon juice just before serving.

quick crumbed broccoli

Preheat oven to 190°C/170°C fan forced. Spray broccoli florets with olive oil and roast until tender. Sprinkle with a mixture of toasted panko breadcrumbs, shredded parmesan and sweet paprika.

mini cheese & artichoke tarts

Make these for starters. Steam Jerusalem artichokes until tender. Thinly slice. Sauté in butter and fresh thyme leaves. Cut rounds of puff pastry. Layer with slices of artichoke. Bake until golden. Sprinkle with shaved parmesan and thyme leaves.

lemon blinis

Try this as a side with chicken or lamb. Thinly slice 1 lemon. Pour 2 tbs pancake batter into a non-stick frying pan over medium-low heat. Top with 1 lemon slice. Sprinkle with ½ tsp caster sugar. Flip. Cook until lemon is caramelised and pancake is cooked through.

borlotti beans

Let the flavour of borlotti beans shine for your next side dish. Simply peel, pod and cook in boiling water. Drain and drizzle with olive oil, toss in fresh chopped parsley and season.

citrus salsa

Try this zesty salsa! Peel and chop tangelos. Mix with finely chopped red onion, chopped fresh coriander and finely chopped fresh chilli. Stir in a dash of olive oil.

BEAUTIFUL BEETS

For a healthy salad, just peel and coarsely grate fresh beetroot, then toss with chopped orange segments and tamari almonds and serve dressed with honey and olive oil.

winter salad

Finely shred young silverbeet leaves. Toss with thinly sliced red onion, drained canned chickpeas and toasted walnuts. Dress with olive oil and lemon juice.

curried parsnips

Slice parsnips lengthways. Roast until golden. Mix curry paste with softened butter and dollop over parsnips.

FRESH SIDES

241

" Fresh flavours combine to create no-fuss starters, zingy salads, delicious roasted vegies and herb-laden buttered potatoes. "

GRAPEFRUIT SALAD SPIN

Get fresh with this simple salad! Lay rounds of pink or red grapefruit on a plate, then top with baby rocket and sliced avocado. Dress with a lemon vinaigrette and sprinkle with toasted pine nuts.

balsamic onions

Preheat oven to 180°C/160°C fan forced. Quarter red onions, keeping the bases intact. Place in a snug baking dish with bay leaves. Drizzle with extra virgin olive oil and balsamic vinegar. Season. Bake for 45 minutes or until tender, then serve as a hearty side.

rosemary butter

Combine finely chopped fresh rosemary with softened butter and crushed garlic. Toss with roasted kipfler potatoes to make a simple accompaniment for slow-cooked lamb, beef or pork.

easy beans

Need a no-fuss starter idea? Pod and simmer borlotti beans until tender. Toss with extra virgin olive oil, lemon juice and fresh herbs. Serve on chargrilled bread with grilled zucchini ribbons, parmesan and a drizzle of oil.

cheesy sprouts

Drizzle halved brussels sprouts with olive oil. Roast on a lined baking tray at 180°C/160°C fan forced until crisp. Add grated parmesan and roast for 5 more minutes. Serve with lemon wedges alongside slow-cooked beef.

easy taters

herbed carrots
Place washed and dried carrots in an oven bag with a knob of butter, chopped garlic and fresh thyme leaves. Roast until golden.

hot potatoes
Peel potatoes and trim into a neat oval shape. Trim one end so they sit flat. Heat a little oil and butter in a frying pan and place the potatoes standing up in the pan. Cover with stock. Cook until stock is absorbed and base of potatoes are golden and crisp. Sprinkle with sea salt and micro herbs.

fast buks
We love this healthy side! Just halve and chargrill baby buk choy until tender crisp. Drizzle with oyster sauce and a splash of soy. Scatter with sliced chilli and toasted sesame seeds.

Remove inner stems from silverbeet leaves. Blanch in boiling water and roll up with rice salad for a light side dish.

APPLE SALAD

Cut a red Delicious apple into wedges. Pan-fry with sliced haloumi until golden. Drizzle with honey, top with chopped toasted macadamias, and serve on a bed of baby spinach leaves.

cauliflower power

Deep fry cauliflower florets until golden. Drizzle with Greek yoghurt. Sprinkle with toasted pinenuts.

ginger spice

For a spicy caramel sauce, simmer freshly grated ginger with brown sugar, butter and cream.

INDEX

OUR COMPREHENSIVE INDEX LISTS RECIPES
BY PREP TIME, KEY GUIDE AND MAIN INGREDIENT.

Slow Cooker
INDEX BY PREP TIME

Here are recipes you can throw together in the slow cooker before work, plus some that take a little longer to prepare, for a richer and more nuanced flavour.

Rushing to get out the door? Choose your recipe by the prep time needed.

5 MINUTES

Cambodian curry with coconut	150
Poached raspberry pears	228
Pulled pork with chilli	20
Pulled vegies in tortillas	94

10 MINUTES

Cauliflower korma	142
Chicken diane with fettuccine	168
Chicken with pesto butter	22
Coconut beef curry with pumpkin	146
Creamy butter chicken	154
French-style soup with chicken	62
Lentil soup with cheese toast	72
Middle Eastern chickpea stew	114
Pork ribs with smoked spices	194
Red lentil broth	60
Roast beef with horseradish	46
Slow-cooker beef daube	130
Slow-cooker beef teriyaki	98
Soup with ham and lentils	66
Southern pork ribs	210
Sweet potato curry with beef	152
Turkey fettuccine cacciatore	172
Tuscan-style ribollita	68
Vegetable harira	52

15 MINUTES

Apple cinnamon French toast	216
Apricot chicken tagine	96
Beef and barley soup	76
Cheesy garlic pull-apart	204
Chicken and chorizo gumbo	126
Chicken and mushroom stroganoff	106
Chicken curry with mango	134
Chickpea soup with lamb	54
Classic apricot chicken	92

Classic roast beef and vegies	38
Classic Vietnamese bo kho	112
Creamy vegetarian 'bake'	192
Easiest-ever satay pork	138
Honeyed apricot lamb with couscous	40
Italian beef with gnocchi	90
Lamb soup with pumpkin	80
Lamb with almond and pomegranate	188
Massaman beef and potato	140
Mexican chicken soup with corn	74
No-fuss pork with lemon sage	42
Pork and veal meatball rigatoni	162
Pulled turkey with pineapple	102
Quinoa salad with citrus lamb	182
Rustic Italian chicken casserole	100
Slow-baked apples	232
Slow-cooker beef goulash	118
Slow-cooker chorizo frittata	200
Spice-rubbed turkey	18
Spicy black bean bowl	70
Spinach and ricotta cannelloni	164
Sweet potato soup with harissa	64
Vegetarian minestrone	56
Vegie curry with chickpeas	148

20 MINUTES

Apple and rhubarb cobbler	218
Beef and Guinness brisket	24
Beef and lemongrass pot roast	16
Beef brisket bourguignon	88
Caramel pork with Asian greens	122
Cheesy potato with fennel	196
Cinnamon and vanilla quinces	224
Corned beef with cider	32
Cuban pulled beef	104
Dumplings with salted caramel	214
French Burgundy beef	124

Giant golden syrup dumpling	230
Greek pork with chickpeas	26
Lamb chops in red wine	44
Lamb shanks with Guinness	108
Lamb with beetroot hummus	36
Mexican spiced pork and salsa	178
Middle Eastern lamb with hummus	30
Middle Eastern stuffed capsicums	202
Moroccan beef and barley	116
Nyonya chicken curry	144
Pea and ham soup	58
Pickled veg with miso eggplant	206
Pork and pineapple rice bowl	186
Pork with sage and apple	48
Raspberry scrolls	222
Shredded chicken with lime	176
Sicilian pot roast with veal	128
Upside-down mandarin pudding	220

25 MINUTES OR MORE

Bean soup with pancetta	82
Cabbage rolls with lemon sauce	208
Chorizo salad with prawns	184
Duck ragu with pappardelle	166
Easy home-style lasagna	160
Hummingbird cake	226
Indian-style beef roast	28
Lamb raan with minted rice	34
Lentil and barley salad	180
Massaman lamb shanks	156
Pomegranate lamb shanks	86
Ribs with rosemary cauliflower	198
Slow beef pho bo	78
Slow-cooked coq au vin	120
Slow-cooked mavrou	136
Spicy chicken meatballs	110
Vegetarian lentil lasagne	170

Slow Cooker
INDEX BY KEY GUIDE

All of the recipes in this book are Make Ahead, for your convenience.
Here's a list of some other key features.

Slow Cooker
INDEX BY MAIN INGREDIENT

Vegetarian or omnivore, check this index for your
protein preference, to make shopping and cooking easier.

CREDITS

editor-in-chief Brodee Myers
brodee.myerscooke@news.com.au
group commissioning editor Cassie Mercer
food director Michelle Southan
book food editor Tracy Rutherford
magazine food editors Alison Adams, Gemma Luongo
creative director Giota Letsios
art director Natasha Barisa
chief subeditor Alex McDivitt
subeditors Lynne Testoni, Melody Lord
design concept Rachelle Napper, Brush Media
book art director Chi Lam
nutrition editor Chrissy Freer
editorial coordinator Elizabeth Hayes

managing director, News DNA Julian Delany
director of FoodCorp Fiona Nilsson

HarperCollinsPublishers** Australia**
publishing director Brigitta Doyle
head of Australian non-fiction Helen Littleton

COVER IMAGES

Guy Bailey, Chris L Jones, Nigel Lough

CONTRIBUTORS

Recipes

Alison Adams, Emma Braz, Claire Brookman, Kim Coverdale, Dixie Elliot, Chrissy Freer, Amira Georgy, Marion Grasby, Jessica Holmes, Kirrily la Rosa, Cathie Lonnie, Gemma Luongo, Liz Macri, Louise Patniotis, Miranda Payne, Angela Portela, Kerrie Ray, Tracy Rutherford, Dominic Smith, Katrina Woodman, Jo-Anne Woodman

Photography

Guy Bailey, Chris L Jones, Vanessa Levis, Nigel Lough, Amanda McLauchlan, Cath Muscat, Mark O'Meara, Rob Palmer, Al Richardson, Jeremy Simons, Brett Stevens, Craig Wall, Andrew Young

HarperCollins*Publishers*

Australia • Brazil • Canada • France • Germany • Holland
• Hungary • India • Italy • Japan • Mexico • New Zealand
• Poland • Spain • Sweden • Switzerland • United Kingdom
• United States of America

First published in Australia in 2020
by HarperCollins*Publishers* Australia Pty Limited
ABN 36 009 913 517
harpercollins.com.au

A catalogue record for this book is available
from the National Library of Australia

ISBN 978 1 4607 5899 1 (paperback)
ISBN 978 1 4607 1286 3 (ebook)

Colour reproduction by Graphic Print Group, South Australia
Printed and bound in China by RR Donnelley

8,7 6 5 4 3 2 1   20 21 22 23

THANK YOU

At taste.com.au HQ, we're crazy for slow cookers. And *Ultimate Slow Cooker* is a product of all those recipes we love cooking – year round, come hail or shine. We'd like to thank everyone on the team who contributed their expertise to this book – from our foodies to design, the sub editors to the digital team. Each recipe is a result of their amazing passion and teamwork.

A huge thank you as well to Brigitta Doyle and Helen Littleton, our partners-in-crime at HarperCollins. You helped us bring this book alive and we're very thankful for your expertise.

We'd also like to thank... you, the audience of taste.com.au! Thousands of passionate cooks visit our site every day to plan, cook and share their reviews, ratings and recipe twists and tips. We love hearing about your passion for cooking and the gusto with which you make our recipes, so keep those reviews, comments and photos coming.

Music Theory Practice Papers 2017

Adapted from the 2017 Music Theory
exam papers

ABRSM Grade 1

Includes new
question types
in use from
2018

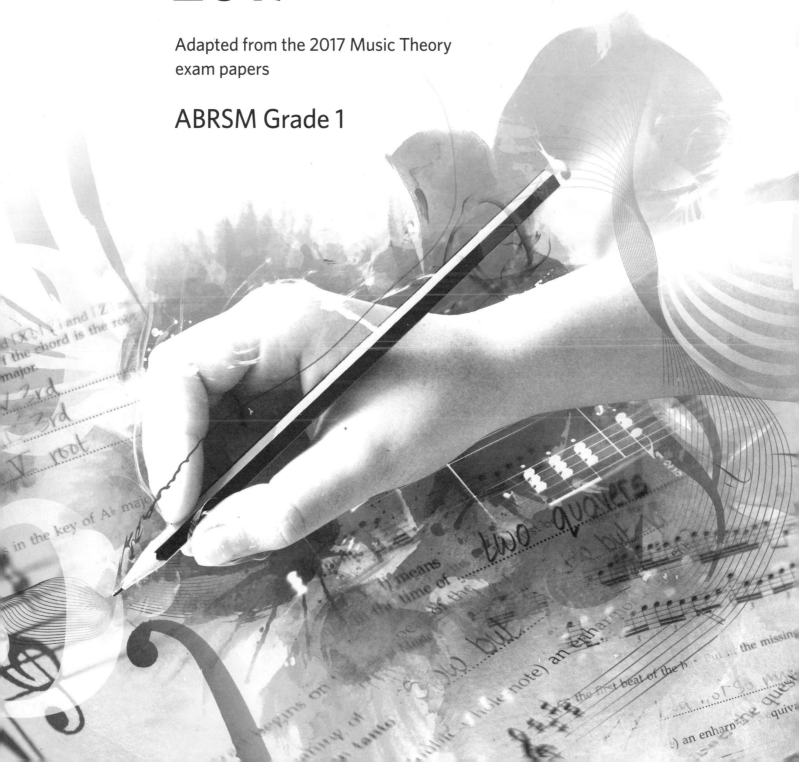

Music Theory Practice Papers 2017

ABRSM's *Music Theory Practice Papers 2017* are adapted from the 2017 Music Theory exam papers. Some questions are the same as those used in recent exams. Others have been adapted to reflect the new question types being used in some parts of the Grade 1 to 5 papers from 1 January 2018. These include multiple-choice questions for some terms and signs and questions with a clearer layout.

The *Music Theory Practice Papers 2017* for Grades 1 to 5 do not include rhythm-writing, word-setting, melody-writing or SATB short/open score questions, as these no longer appear in exams.

Music Theory exams – Grades 1 to 5, from 1 January 2018

Although we have made some small changes to Music Theory exams at Grades 1 to 5, the knowledge needed by candidates remains the same. ABRSM's existing music theory books continue to be valid and useful resources for candidates preparing for exams.

Find out more about our Grade 1 to 5 Music Theory exams at **www.abrsm.org/theory**.

© 2018 by The Associated Board of the Royal Schools of Music
Published by ABRSM (Publishing) Ltd, a wholly owned subsidiary of ABRSM
Cover by Kate Benjamin & Andy Potts
Printed in England by Halstan & Co. Ltd, Amersham, Bucks, on materials from sustainable sources